2H
1is

SPIRIT and STRUGGLE in Southern ASIA

Edited by Barbara H. Chase and Martha L. Man

ISBN 0-377-00157-0
Editorial Offices: 475 Riverside Drive, Room 772,
New York, NY 10115
Distribution Offices: P.O. Box 37844, Cincinnati, OH 45237
Copyright © 1986 Friendship Press, Inc.
Printed in the. United States of America

CONTENTS

PREFACE

From Nepal's Himalayan peaks to the rain forests of Sri Lanka, currents of life in southern Asia flow into one another and diverge. The region is home to one in five people in the world. Hundreds of languages and dialects are spoken; dozens of distinct cultural traditions are expressed; all of the world's major religions are practiced.

Each of the five countries in this study—Bangladesh, India, Nepal, Pakistan and Sri Lanka—has been profoundly affected by the cultures of its indigenous peoples as well as by a history of interventions from countries outside the region. Today, each one is an independent nation with its own political structure, economy, national aspirations and social tensions. Yet across the vast subcontinent the intensity of people's spirit and their struggle to hold onto their identities despite outside influences continue to bind southern Asians together.

This study is arranged in such a way that North American readers will be able to examine the same subject from different southern Asian perspectives. The areas covered are: history, religion, the role of women, culture, peace, justice and militarization. The contributors to the book are church leaders and educators, activists and poets, men and women, famous sages and anonymous young people. Through their analyses, reflections, stories and outcries the reader is challenged to exchange his or her old perceptions of southern Asia for new understanding, and to make a serious response to what this region's history and current situation tell us about our world.

DIVERTED STREAMS OF HISTORY

Introduction

Over the centuries, the development of southern Asian nations and cultures has been deeply affected—one might even say diverted—by political events. In Sri Lanka, for example, Britain brought Tamils and Sinhalese together in a new way for its own economic purposes. The result has been violent racial tensions that have torn apart this island nation. How can mutual trust and interdependence between Tamils and Sinhalese be restored in an atmosphere of continuing violence? India's independence from Britain in 1947 established it as the world's largest democracy. The implementation of this democracy has, however, been repeatedly blocked by political, religious and racial injustices. While the 1984 assassination of Prime Minister Indira Gandhi brought some of these injustices to light, it remains to be seen how decisively it affected the flow of India's history. Partition from India in 1947 created Pakistan as the world's first Islamic nation. Unfortunately, today in Pakistan there is extensive militarization (the increasing influence of military institutions on civilian society). Pakistan is surrounded by the Soviet Union, China, India, Afghanistan and Iran. It has tried to establish social, political and educational systems to undergird an Islamic way of life. Amid all this, Pakistan has accepted over three million Afghan refugees who may remain in the country for decades to come. Partition was a traumatic event for Bangladesh as well as for Pakistan and India. Bangladeshis not only had to deal with partition, however; they had to endure the civil war to which it led them. Impoverished by internal strife, Bangladesh is also the frequent victim of devastating droughts and floods. Throughout the history of foreign intervention and its aftermath that have beset her neighbors, Nepal has moved slowly from an isolationism imposed to preserve her cultural identity to the acceptance of twentieth century development.

INDIA
A Democracy Keeps Life Going
by G. R. Karat

What happened on the forenoon of October 31 [1984] at 1, Saf-darjung Road, New Delhi, was murder most foul. If it is said to be part of modern-day politics—as it sometimes appears to be—we had better hand over politics to sharpshooters. If a deep sense of religious outrage is cited in mitigation of it, it is time to declare that true religion of any brand had nothing to do with it. No religion that demands such bloody vendetta for safeguarding its own honor deserves a place in civilized, multi-religious communities. If the shock and grief of the nation at the murder of Mrs. Gandhi were indeed the manifestation of its humane conscience and not mere ritualistic reaction to death in high places, then it is time Indians of all castes, colors and creeds took a critical look at the politics and religion that their national life has been promoting these many years. It is an ominous fact that in our times the various religions have served to paint politics largely red with blood in many parts of the world.

When the tragic news broke on me that mid-day of October 31 in Singapore, my mind went back to some of the other notable deaths in India since Independence. I remember the evening in Madras when the news of Gandhiji's assassination came over the wireless. I was just setting out for an evening walk . . . I was stunned. A strange fear and heavy despair seized my heart. I returned to my room in the YMCA hostel, fell on my knees by my bed and prayed, incoherent with tears. The feeling uppermost in my mind was that we as a nation did not deserve anything good after what had happened. I prayed for God's mercy and forgiveness for me and for my country. I remember, too, how in the midst of the pervading sense of tragedy, there was profound relief that a Muslim was not responsible for the dastardly murder. The nightmares of the killings that followed the Partition were still green in everybody's memory.

I was traveling in a crowded train somewhere in [the state of]

From an article in the November 15, 1984 issue of CCA News. *G.R. Karat, editor of* CCA News, *is secretary for communications of the Christian Conference of Asia.*

Andhra Pradesh on SCM [Student Christian Movement] business when I heard the news of Nehru's death. We knew he was ailing, and so deep sadness rather than shock was the reaction on the railway train. Nehru meant so much to people of my generation. His patient integrity, his eloquence, the quality of his mind and life that set him apart even among the other formidable leaders of the freedom struggle, made us proud to be citizens of India. Of course for some time before his death people had begun to ask the question, Who after Nehru? Though we might have been hard put to answer it with an incontestable name, we were not panicking. The reservoir of political leadership was still fairly full. We felt that ultimately we would come through. The choice and the all-too-brief record of Lal Bahadur Shastri as Nehru's successor amply vindicated the resilience and health of our democracy.

Two years later I was at breakfast at my home in SCM House, Banglalore. A young student friend rushed in with the news that Shastri had died at Tashkent. I had begun to admire him. The diminutive, home-grown, ascetic prime minister was so very different from the patrician Nehru, and yet he had grown fast and visibly to fill worthily what was thought to be Goliath's armor. One of the acid tests of democracy that most Third World democracies fail is the democratization of leadership. I felt that with Shastri we had broken the spell of elitism, and so I have never ceased wondering about the ways of God and man that gave him such short innings and let India's future be mortgaged to the future of the Nehru dynasty.

When yet another of his reckless and illegal stunts killed Sanjay Gandhi I was in the United Kingdom. I was sorry a fellow human being had died needlessly. My heart went out to the young widow and orphaned son and to the grieving mother, but I felt no sense of loss. In fact, I could not help thinking that his death was good for the country because I saw no other way anyone could have rid us of him and saved India from his politics of banditry. Even his fond and mighty mother seemed determined to bequeath it to the nation after her.

My feelings about Indira Gandhi's death have been more complex. I am not inclined to join in all the breast-beating that is going on around me, but I am truly sorry she is dead and killed the way she was killed—by an amalgam of communal and religious fervor, betrayal of a trust which she dared to repose in her security men against all common sense and prudence, a combination of cool calculation and murderous frenzy which mowed down an unsuspecting, unarmed woman just when and where she had every right to feel safe. Further, it has been my belief that India's growth to maturity and effectiveness as a democracy of the people lay in our learning to cope with Indira through political processes and not through a pistol.

3

Mrs. Gandhi was undoubtedly one of the most remarkable women of our times, nationally and internationally. As prime minister she was probably the only Indian leader of truly national eminence. Controversy or condemnation of the paths she chose to reach and retain that eminence never seemed to deter her. Her will to power was indefatigable, frightening. She was unstoppable. She earned a large measure of credibility for her position because she was proud of India and made it count in international affairs. She successfully projected herself as the guardian not only of the frontiers of the country but also of its democratic, socialist and secular character, of its many minorities and its rural masses.

Her son is now heir to all this, and he would be expected to preserve these because most thoughtful Indians are no less committed to them. India's misery is that in spite of this its politics is sterile—contentious, divisive, devoid of commitment to any great national purpose and code of honor. Therefore it would seem that Rajiv Gandhi's task is not so much to mummify his inheritance as to transform it. We must hope and pray that, whether he stays for a long or short period in his enormously powerful position as prime minister, Rajiv Gandhi will act with courage and a new vision, remembering that what he has been called to tend is India primarily and not its prime ministership.

PAKISTAN
Refugees or Kin?

For many Pakistanis, the flood of refugees from Afghanistan is a family matter with international dimensions—one that stirs memories of their own country's turbulent history.

At the Khyber Pass, Northwest Frontier Province, the night's darkness came quickly. The shopkeeper had just finished lighting the small lamps when he heard outside his shop the muffled sound of another group of refugees from Afghanistan. He recognized the dragging steps of the children, the hesitant pace of the elders and the bleating of sheep. How many sheep with this group? Did they have any possessions with them, or had they fled their village so quickly they had nothing? These days the road was never empty. Even the cold weather had not stopped the traffic, for many refugees were hurrying to beat the winter snows which would make the journey virtually impossible. He wondered if any of his relatives would be in this group. The Pushtu community had never paid much attention to the national borders governments proclaimed. Relatives were relatives, kin to be cared for, not enemies or foreigners from another country.

Just as the tea water was ready, a family appeared in the doorway seeking warmth and food. It had been a long journey, but the family felt relieved to have crossed the Khyber Pass with little incident and to be on Pakistani soil. The tea was worth the few *takas* they had left. The shopkeeper showed them where they could spend the night and said that in the morning he would point the way to a transit camp where they would find blankets, tents, food and water while waiting to get into a permanent refugee camp. As the women and children found their sleeping places the men stayed up to share the latest news of the conflict between the government of Afghanistan, which continued to receive large-scale Soviet support, and the guerrilla fighters of Afghanistan.

Written by Barbara H. Chase, using background material in "Afghan Refugees in Pakistan: Will They Go Home Again?" published by the U.S. Committee for Refugees, New York (December 1982) and other general resources on Pakistan.

The shopkeeper rose early the next morning. He reflected on the millions of people from Afghanistan who were now in his country. The latest government reports said that more than three million were now living here. He could believe it! This route was a major one, although at the worst of times the refugees crossed over at other points. As Muslims, they had a natural understanding with each other; as Pushtu, they were kin. The shopkeeper was pleased that his country was doing so much.

He remembered the time when most of the people in Pakistan had been refugees. He and his people had lived in this territory for centuries, but he recalled how, in 1947, millions had moved to newly-created West Pakistan from India; they had no intention of returning to India. Others feared remaining in West Pakistan, the first officially Islamic nation in the world, and rushed to India, only to find that there they, too, had to adjust to an entirely new way of life. He shuddered as he remembered those times and looked compassionately at those who came from Afghanistan. At least many of them came with the hope of returning someday.

Back in 1947, the shopkeeper recalled, he and his people had wondered what this new Islamic nation called the Republic of Pakistan would mean to them. There was a special pride in being an Islamic nation. Under the present regime of General Zia, the *mullahs* (priests) were finally having more to say about interpreting the *shariat* (laws). He understood that those who were not Muslim might have problems with them, such as the Hindus of the Sind area and the Christians. But Islam was a compassionate faith and surely some accommodation could be worked out for these people.

As the refugee family gathered their few possessions and sheep together and got ready to leave, the shopkeeper gave them directions to the transit camp. He knew that they would use their time in the transit camp to try to find out what camp other relatives were in, and then join them there. Families wanted to be reunited with each other; that was even more important than being officially registered so that housing and food supplies could be allocated. With no barbed wire and no restriction on their movement it was possible for refugees to roam the countryside to find their relatives.

Being on the main trade and communication route between Pakistan and Afghanistan, the shopkeeper had learned a number of languages. Sometimes, instead of a refugee family, he would find a foreign correspondent in his shop, asking for an interview. Would he answer a few questions? But the shopkeeper found their questions strange, such as: *Why do you Pakistanis accept all these Afghan refugees? Aren't you afraid they will stay forever?* Why couldn't these foreigners understand we are the same people, divided by meaningless borders? Why couldn't they understand that as an Islamic nation we are bound to care for our Muslim friends and neighbors?

A better question to him was: *How has the influx of refugees affected*

Pakistan's neverending conflict with India? India is Pakistan's biggest threat, the shopkeeper would reply. With her large army and her nuclear expertise, she continues to threaten us. We have even had to use our scarce resources for nuclear development.

They asked, *How are Pakistanis affected by the influx of the Afghan refugees?* As President Zia says in the papers, our faith demands that we care for our Afghan neighbors, the shopkeeper would reply. He agreed with this. They could do no less. But he was beginning to hear grumbling from many Pakistanis who were critical of military control, and of international support like that of the U.S., which aided that control. Then there were those who felt the Pakistani government was giving more to the refugees than to them! Some shepherds complained that wasn't enough land for their own herds. Firewood was becoming scarce. The price of petrol and cooking oil was too high. These are real problems, but what can we do? he thought. They are our neighbors, our kin.

The foreign reporters kept asking him questions like: *Aren't you afraid of supporting Afghan refugees? Aren't you afraid of retaliation from the Soviet Union?* How to answer this? Pakistan was surrounded by large and powerful nations: the Soviet Union, China, India, Iran. This was their reality. This was nothing new. By doing the honorable thing they had the support of many countries, particularly Islamic countries, and they found strength in developing these ties.

Does Pakistan have the leadership to take care of over three million refugees for decades to come? How could he explain to these foreigners Pakistani pride at being Pakistani? Perhaps if they understood the Qu'ran they could understand Pakistan. The shopkeeper remembered the midnight broadcast on the 15th of August, 1947, when over the radio in Urdu came the reciting of the opening verses of *Sura Fat-h* (Victory) of the Holy Quran and how he had felt hope for the future:

> Verily We have granted
> Thee a manifest Victory:
> That God may forgive thee
> Thy faults of the past
> And those to follow;
> Fulfill his Favor to thee;
> And guide thee
> On the Straight Way;
> And that God may help
> Thee with powerful help.

From an English translation of The Holy Qu'ran, by Abdullah Yusuf Ali.

BANGLADESH
"Where is Deliverance to be Found?"

Once East Pakistan, Bangladesh continues to be beset by poverty, the ravages of war and weather. In the following story, a young Bangladeshi seeks a vocation that will enable him to help his country.

Here is thy footstool and there rest thy feet

Where live the poorest, and lowliest, and lost.

When I try to bow to thee, my obeisance cannot reach
down to the depth where thy feet rest among the poorest,
and lowliest, and lost.

Pride can never approach to where thou walkest in the clothes
of the humble among the poorest, and lowliest, and lost.

My heart can never find its way to where thou keepest
company with the companionless among the poorest,
the lowliest, and the lost.*

Hassim recited these words for what seemed like the hundredth time. Here he was with the future ahead of him, with an opportunity to study, to do meaningful work . . . all he had worked, hoped and dreamed for. Why did he hesitate? He wondered if his father and his grandfather had wrestled with such decisions.

Hassim had been about eight years old during the terrible civil war of liberation which had brought Bangladesh into existence in 1971. He knew how blessed he had been. He had been spared. Not so his two older sisters and two older brothers. Gone. Massacred. Shot in cross-fire between the Liberation Army and the Pakistani Army. His sisters . . . oh, the thought of their death was still almost more than he could bear. To die so young in their

*From *Gitanjali*, by Rabindranath Tagore.

Written by Barbara H. Chase, using general background material on Bangladesh, in particular, Pro Mundi Vita: Dossiers: "Bangladesh: A Test-Case for a Self-reliant Nation and a Church," *(Brussels: Pro Mundi Vita, August, 1979) and* Gitanjali, *by Rabindranath Tagore (New Delhi: MacMillan, 1983; first printed in 1913).*

blossoming teenage years was bad enough, but to know they had been raped stirred him to tears even fourteen years later. Someone told him it was a blessing that his sisters had died because they would have been outcasts if they had lived. He found this even more difficult to understand.

In school he had studied the civil war and the 1947 Partition that had created East and West Pakistan. He had heard his grandfather's stories about that terrible time of struggle between Partition and Liberation. His grandfather was a scholar of Bengali poets. He had been astounded by West Pakistan's pronouncement, after Partition, that Urdu was to be the national language and Arabic the official script. His very soul had been punctured by the thought of giving up the Bengali language. This was what had given his life meaning and gave meaning to the Bengali people. His strong feelings for his language led him to become involved in the political struggle. This was not his usual way.

Hassim's father had been nine years old at the time of the 1947 Partition. He knew little about it until the issue of language became a topic of daily conversation in their home. He had little interest in Bengali poetry or literature; he wanted to be a businessman. As a Christian in a Muslim country, this would not be easy. But the Catholic church had provided Hassim's father with schooling. He completed high school and afterwards, went to work on a jute plantation. Jute was Pakistan's major export in those early years after Partition and the job was good; he was promoted to supervisor. He learned much about jute and its products, like gunny sacks and rope, that were needed around the world. But he also feared the yearly monsoons and droughts that could wipe out a crop if it was not already harvested. The cycle of droughts and floods seemed to be the cycle of life for them all.

While Hassim's grandfather opposed the imposition of Urdu as the national language, his father was beginning to wonder why Pakistan was not receiving just returns on their exports of jute. It had been difficult, those first years after Partition, because the jute mills that processed the raw jute were in Calcutta. Businessmen from West Pakistan invested funds for the creation of Pakistani mills, so the industry was thriving. But the returned benefits to his own region, East Pakistan, never adequately materialized.

The feeling of oppression, of injustice, grew and grew. Neither of the two men were interested, at first, in the Aswami League, but they learned that this group expounded just what they thought. They felt comradeship with these Muslims who felt the same way they did. Around this time Hassim's father began to read Tagore. In fact, it had been his own father who had given Hassim this poem which haunted him. It had touched his grandfather, his father, and now it was penetrating his own being as he made his decision for the future.

The barbaric violence of the civil war was something neither his father nor his grandfather talked about much. It was his mother who, haunted by it all, tried to help Hassim understand the Bengali people's frustration and rage. His mother found solace in her church so she insisted that young Hassim go to catechism, take his first communion, be an altar boy, attend school regularly, and now she was looking for a young girl for him to marry. She longed for grandchildren to love and to replace those lost to her.

What would she think of the offer the church had made to him? For Hassim had also found solace in the church. He had found strength and stability in the answers the church provided in the face of so much stress and uncertainty. Ironically, it was the church which had sent him as a representative to an ecumenical youth meeting. And it was at this meeting that he had begun to question the direction of his life.

During one of the worship times, someone had read the poem by Tagore. He had been sure he knew what it meant, but in this worship service the entire group had been challenged to follow its teachings! The leader had read Tagore's poem along with Jesus' admonition to feed the hungry, clothe the naked, visit the sick and those in prison. He had asked: "What will your response be? The poorest, the lowliest, the lost are right here in our town, in our country. People from around the world provide relief and reha- bilitation, but what are we Bengalis doing? What are we Bengali Christians doing? Do we have to be paid by others to take care of our own? *What will your response be?*"

Hassim continued to be in touch with some members of that group. They tried to understand why their country could be called a "basket case" by someone like Dr. Henry Kissinger. Was it true that they were a "disabled" country, to be permanently carried on the backs of the rest of the world? If so (and they would not yet acknowledge that fact!) was there not something they could do about it? Each participant at that ecumenical youth meeting had returned to his or her own local church and asked such questions of the sisters and the priests. Most had felt rebuffed, had been told that such questions were not the concern of the church. Each one confessed to feeling frustrated, but more and more determined.

And now the time for his personal decision had come. He, Has- sim must answer the church's invitation to become a priest. A college education and a vocation of service to the people were offered to him. He knew that a positive response would at first break his mother's heart but that in the end she would be proud of him. He wasn't sure how his father and grandfather would feel. They were Christian, but the church was not as much a focal point of their lives as it was for his mother.

Although more than two years had passed since he had been asked for his response "to the poorest, the lowliest," the challenge had never left him. The response of the priests had discouraged him. Would it be possible to serve the poorest and lowliest as a priest? Or as a politician? For his ecumenical youth friends had concluded that no lasting help would come to the poorest of the poor until the government was less corrupt and more responsive to the needs of its people. Was it possible for a Bengali Christian to be elected? Would people believe he was automatically corrupt because he was a politician? The questions seemed to wash over him like a flood and he felt as if he were drowning.

All of a sudden, other words of Tagore came to him—words he knew by heart, words which now had new meaning. His waiting was over. His decision was made. He truly believed that the church would be faithful, that its stance of non-involvement would be transformed, that the church would begin to help to change the structures of Bengali society. Drained from the intensity of his inner struggle, he found himself rising up and nearly shouting Tagore's words:

> Leave this chanting and singing and telling of beads! Whom does thou worship in this lonely dark corner of a temple with doors all shut? Open thine eyes and see thy God is not before thee!

> He is there where the tiller is tilling the hard ground and where the pathmaker is breaking stones. He is with them in sun and in shower, and his garment is covered with dust. Put off thy holy mantle and even like him come down on the dusty soil!

> Deliverance? Where is this deliverance to be found? Our master himself has joyfully taken upon him the bonds of creation: he is bound with us all for ever.

> Come out of thy meditations and leave aside thy flowers and incense! What harm is there if thy clothes become tattered and stained? Meet him and stand by him in toil and in sweat of thy brow.

Why had he limited himself? Why did he think his only options were to become a priest or a politician? He would take that scholarship; he would study economics and education; he would learn why there were poor people; he would learn about international markets and trade; he would find a way for his church to be involved in the life struggles of the people. The specific job he would do was not certain, but the commitment to getting at the structures which imprisoned minds, bodies and spirits was aflame!

NEPAL
No Longer a Bird
with Clipped Wings

What comes to your mind when you think of Nepal? A picture of magnificent mountains? The famous Gurkhaj soldiers who fought under British command during the Second World War? Did desire to know more about the birds of the world introduce you to their isolated habitats through the explorations of missionary Robert Fleming? Are you one of the fortunate travelers who has made a stopover in Kathmandu? Or, if your denomination is a member of the United Mission to Nepal,* have you received first-hand accounts of the developments in that land?

Whatever your source of information, you would probably admit that it is slanted from a foreigner's perspective. One reason is that when Nepalese write about their country, they write in Nepali for their own people; when translated, these writings naturally reveal the interests of the translator. As one seeks knowledge from the Nepali people themselves, it becomes evident how much isolation has affected the flow of information between Nepal and the rest of the world.

From about 1846 to 1951, Nepal was ruled by the Ranas, a family of hereditary prime ministers who pursued a policy of close cooperation with the British in India. In the late 1880's, when the British were expanding, they were seen by Nepalese leaders as an illegitimate empire overrunning the territory. After a series of clashes between the British and the Gorkhalis, of the kingdom of Gorkha, about one-third of Nepali territory closest to India, was annexed to British India. The Nepalese lost this region, but the manner in which they had resisted gained them British India's respect.

Seeing how Europeans operated in India and other parts of Asia convinced the mountain people of Nepal that the best defense was

*See page 25.

Written by Barbara H. Chase from background material in Nepal and the Gospel of God, *by Jonathan Lindell (published by the United Mission to Nepal in collaboration with Masihi Sahitya Sanstha, 1979) and from Norma Kehrberg's unpublished manuscript, "Nepali Songs: Personal Perspective of Two Contemporary Artists."*

complete isolation. No one was allowed to come into their land. "This was supported by the Brahmins, who also wanted to see their country and society remain pure and free from defilements of foreign presence and ways."[1] It was further supported by the viewpoint that if any trade was to pass through Nepal it should be handled entirely by Nepalese, thus keeping the profits within the country as well as keeping out questionable strangers. Until a 1923 treaty, not even Indian traders were allowed to stay overnight in Nepal.

While Nepal was keeping foreigners out, India was controlling Nepal's foreign relations, for as long as the British ruled India no foreigner could enter Nepal without permission of the British Government in India.[2]

As the years passed the Nepalese people began to resemble a bird with clipped wings, unable to take flight into the future, unable to escape the cage they had built. The Gurkhaj soldiers, however, had the advantage of traveling quite widely. They saw what being open to the world could mean to Nepal. Such soldiers became part of the Nepal Congress Party which, in 1951, began agitating for a more open and democratic government. This led to revolution, and the royal line, represented by King Tribhuvan, returned to power.

The general election held in 1959 resulted in an overwhelming victory for the Congress Party, but this only lasted until the end of 1960 when King Mahendra, who had succeeded Tribhuvan, dismissed his ministers and inaugurated his personal rule. Mahendra died in 1972 and was succeeded by his son, Birendra, who was crowned in 1975. Four years later, Birendra announced that the political system would be put to a vote and on May 2, 1980 a referendum was held. The result was a narrow victory for continuation of the two-decades-old *panchayat* system of government. The *panchayat* system, based on the principal of five elders in a local village, is now practiced at the regional and national level.

After decades of isolation Nepal is trying to understand her resources and to use them to shape a more progressive country. Jonathan Lindell compares the country to a "lump of clay swiftly turning on the wheel" of a potter. "The vessel of old Nepal is broken; a new Nepal is being formed. Many hands are on that clay, with many interests. There are business hands and religious hands, educated hands and common hands, each contributing its shape to the lump. His Majesty has his hands strongly on the clay, together with the many members of his government. Nepal is in the making."[3]

Norma Kehrberg shares the following story, which may help us understand the dilemma of people as they shake off their isolation and take responsibility for the development of their country.

One cold morning in a small bazaar on the outskirts of Kathmandu, the poet Manjul met a shivering, half-clothed old man.

Manjul offered to buy him a cup of hot tea. The old man replied, "Will you save my life by giving me one cup of tea? If you want to save my life, you must also save the lives of all those distressful ones whose lives are passing through the world like a flowing river." Manjul was a bit frightened to hear this, but he followed the old man throughout the city, listening to his words:

A million men have died,
A million men live
Life is destroyed within my memory
But life goes on.

The old man was none other than the great Nepalese poet, Laxmi Prashad Devkota.[4]

"But life goes on." And Nepal is opening its doors, its borders, cautiously, hesitantly. Life in Nepal changed forever when her borders were opened in 1951 and not only could the Nepalese see the world beyond, but the world began to see Nepal. From isolation to encounter with new ideas and values, Nepal has become immersed in a unique revolution. As Jonathan Lindell put it: "The basic issues of life, once quiescent, are in heat. Consider, for example, the farmer and his family who lost their house and fields when the highway was cut and blasted through their hillside. The farmer knew and could adjust to the powers of nature in the violence of spring storms, swollen rivers and sudden landslides. But his road came by the purpose of man, in an unholy destruction. In the way he saw it, he and his family drew their life from the soil, like a babe sucks nourishment from his mother's breast. To come and deliberately pitch it down the bank like refuse was beyond his comprehension. It seemed as if the farmer would die in this experience."[5] The question, Who owns the earth and its resources? remains unanswered to this farmer as well as to others sharing the flight of a bird that no longer has clipped wings.

SRI LANKA
The Anguish of a Divided Nation

Sri Lanka today is engulfed by the tragic results of a racial war arising from deep-rooted tensions between the Sinhalese majority and the Tamil minority. Riots in 1958, 1977, 1981 and 1983 have resulted in the killing of hundreds of Tamils, the widespread destruction of property, the creation of large numbers of refugees and displaced people, and repressive government actions. Each community has a different perspective on the situation, as illustrated by the two parts to this section.

Oppression: A Tamil Perspective
by the Rev. Joseph Francis Xavier

On the island of Sri Lanka there are two ethnic groups: the Tamils and the Sinhalese. The Tamils are of Dravidian origin and the Sinhalese of Aryan origin. These two groups have been living in Sri Lanka for over 2000 years, the Tamils mainly in the northern and eastern parts of the island and the Sinhalese occupying the rest of the country. For centuries, thick jungles served as a kind of natural border between the two groups. Prior to the colonial era, the Sinhalese were ruled by their own kings and the Tamils had their own kings.

When Sri Lanka, then known as Ceylon, came under the colonial masters, it was first under the Portuguese, then the Dutch, and finally the British, who, in 1833, unified the country politically. The language of administration was English. During the British period, Tamils from South India were imported for cheap labor to clear the hill country and plant tea. These and their descendants are known as "Tamils of Indian origin".

In 1948, Sri Lanka got its independence. Soon afterwards, "Tamils of Indian origin" were disenfranchised. A few years later, Sinhala was introduced as the only administrative language and ethnic conflicts escalated.

The Rev. Joseph Francis Xavier, a counsellor and psychotherapist, was director of the Counselling Center of Sri Lanka's National Christian Council in Colombo. This section is excerpted from his application, "on humanitarian and compassionate grounds," for landed immigrant status in Canada, where Father Xavier and his family now live in exile.

In 1956, a major communal riot took place in the eastern province. A major outbreak of racial rioting in 1958 led to the beginning of the exodus of Tamils from the rest of the country to the north and the east, which had always been a "homeland" to Tamils—especially to those who had migrated throughout the rest of the country in search of better prospects. Some Tamils of Indian origin returned to India at this time.

Through legislative acts and administrative strategy, the Sinhala government continued to discriminate against Tamils, whose strong identity would not allow them to fall in line with the government's intended process of assimilation. There was discrimination at every level.

Then a Gandhian type of leader arose among the Tamils, Mr. Chelvanayagam. He was a charismatic Christian leader who was unquestioningly accepted by the vast majority of Hindus as well. He proposed a federal form of government, but it was rejected by the Sinhalese majority government. The present president of Sri Lanka, who was at that time in the opposition party, organized massive resistance to Tamil efforts and stirred up the Sinhalese against any kind of federal form of government (which the Sinhala government was prepared at that time to consider).

The charismatic leader of the Tamils united all Tamils politically by forming a party called the Tamil United Liberation Front, which would use only nonviolent methods in the struggle for freedom. In January 1974, Tamil celebrations were deliberately disturbed by police who fired at a live wire; nine Tamils were electrocuted. It is said among Tamils that this was the occasion that moved certain nonviolent Tamil youth to decide to resort to violence, if necessary, in their struggle for freedom.

Early in 1977, the Tamils' charismatic leader died. In July 1977, elections were held. The present president of Sri Lanka and his party won a landslide victory, but for the first time in history, a Tamil became the leader of the opposition party and Tamils voted into parliament members of the Tamil United Liberation Front. In the wake of the elections, racial riots broke out in which thousands of Tamils were left homeless and several were killed. Arson was widespread and there was an unprecedented number of rapes. The people who suffered most were the Tamils of Indian origin who lived in the plantations. This caused many to move towards the north and east or to go back to India.

During these riots I felt it my pastoral duty to take the risk of visiting the riot-torn district of Ratnapura to care for the desperate people there. In the end, the Tamils felt secure enough to return to their homes and Sinhalese volunteered to protect them. Tamils continued, however, to rush into the Vavuniya district to settle in the Tamil areas. It is significant that what the government was trying to avoid was becoming inevitable: the strengthening of the

Tamil "homeland". The state-instigated communal violence was, in fact, defeating its own goals.

Gandhiyam was doing excellent work to help the refugees rehabilitate themselves. Wells were drilled, tractors given to plow the land, medical facilities were made available. A new life began to bloom for these refugees. Village committees were set up. They were able to sell their produce and pay Gandhiyam back for the loans they had obtained. The feeling of being refugees was going away and a new identity was being born.

As the settlements began to grow, the government became disturbed that large numbers of Tamils were coming together. For unknown reasons, nearby Sinhalese villages started trouble, encroaching on the Tamil settlements. Security men threatened Tamil villagers, saying that they would have to return to the plantations.

In July 1982, Dr. Rajasundaram, executive secretary of Gandhiyam, contacted me while I was working in a counseling program in Sarvodaya and invited me to assist him with rehabilitation work. I offered my help to train pre-school teachers, volunteers and staff in developmental psychology, group dynamics, counselling and community development. There was much demand for my work since there were many human problems among the settlers.

At this time accusations were made that certain terrorists who had taken to the jungles had made the Gandhiyam settlements their hideout. There was talk among the Sinhalese police that Gandhiyam was harboring terrorists from the north. In my work with Gandhiyam I never came across anything that would come close to substantiating these allegations. Rajasundaram, I knew, was a busy social worker. He told me that there were efforts to get him in trouble and to discourage the work of Gandhiyam, but kept insisting that I inculcate into my counselling the principle of Gandhian nonviolence and awaken the people's consciousness to become autonomous.

On April 6, 1983, Dr. Rajasundaram, along with several other Gandhiyam leaders, was arrested. At the time I was in Vavuniya. I stayed there and carried on the program, but from then on I seemed a marked person for the government. Soon after the arrest of these leaders, a pattern of harrassment began to threaten the Gandhiyam settlements. Villagers were asked—at the point of a gun—to go back to the plantation areas from which they had come.

I took up their complaints, documented them and wrote letters to government authorities, starting with the president of the country. I also reported the behavior of the police and security forces to the authorities. In Colombo, several Sinhalese leaders and friends rallied round me and we formed the Committee for the Defense of Gandhiyam so that the rehabilitation work it had begun could be continued despite its leaders being in custody.

After this I received threatening telephone calls; anonymous notes in my letterbox informed me that my house would be bombed. One day while I was not at home, five secret-service police came to my home to question my wife about my work in the counselling center and about myself. It is important to mention here that I am married to a Sinhalese who is an English teacher. Two of her brothers are Anglican priests working in Colombo. During the 1977 riots and the 1981 communal violence there were instances in which Sinhalese married to Tamils were attacked and even killed for "betraying their race" by marrying Tamils.

On June 1, 1983 eight Methodist theological students and I were in Vavuniya for a two-day counselling program among the refugees. Twenty miles away there was a shoot-out between security forces and some unknown persons. The eight students and I were arrested—because we were all Tamils, we were told. After questionning at the army camp we were asked to return to the Gandhiyam orphanage where we usually rested after our field work. At midnight I heard the noise of jeeps and saw security service personnel sneaking behind the orphanage. They poured petrol and set fire to the orphanage, then sped off. We fought the fire to save the eighteen little orphans, then we ran into the jungle and hid throughout the night. The next day we returned to the orphanage, which had been reduced to ashes. The police came and took all nine of us to the police station. I was severely disgraced by the police and interrogated for an entire day; they threatened to lock me up but gave no reason for the arrest.

On Thursday, July 21, we heard about a disturbance in Jaffna following the kidnapping of four young women from the teachers training college there. The four had been raped; two of them had committed suicide and the other two were missing. On Saturday the 23rd, some Tamil youths mined a road and ambushed army vehicles and in the shoot-out, thirteen security men were killed.

The next morning, sixteen young Tamil men were pulled out of buses and shot dead by the army as retaliation. About these killings the government-sponsored press carried only the news that thirteen soldiers had been killed by "northern terrorists". This was the occasion that unleashed the terrible pogrom that had been hatched for quite some time as a "final solution to the Tamil problem".

On Sunday night, July 24, communal violence began again with hell-bent fury, simultaneously all across the country. In the city of Colombo, houses of Tamils (according to electoral lists) were burnt down. If Tamils lived in rented houses, the arsonists did not burn the houses but pulled out all their belongings and set them on fire. All Tamil shops and businesses were burned down. Motor vehicles were stopped by large mobs and if there were Tamils in them they were pulled out and attacked; if the vehicle belonged to a Tamil it was set on fire. The death toll reached three hundred by Monday night. My wife witnessed a murder on the road; she saw the madness of the mob setting fire to cars and motorcycles and shops and Tamil establishments. She saw how the mob cheered the police and army vehicles and how the police or soldiers waved back.

The horror that began on Sunday night continued throughout Monday; the president declared a curfew only after the major damage had been done. Near the hill capital of Kandy, several towns were burning; Tamil homes were burning; tens of thousands were left homeless; some died of heart attacks caused by terror and anxiety; there was mourning everywhere.

That night there was horror in Colombo's main prision. Convicted Sinhalese criminals were not locked up in their cells as usual. The room where tools for manual labor were kept was not locked. The Tamil political prisoners were all locked up in their cells. By midnight, the Sinhalese prisoners, as if possessed by demons, moved as a mob on the unarmed Tamil prisoners and tore them to death with crowbars, axes and spears. Thirty-five young Tamil men were done to death in this manner.

The next day the same Sinhalese prisoners again had the freedom to kill, and on that night they killed another seventeen, including Dr. Rajasundaram. He was axed to death.

Threat to my life was now imminent, even from within government circles. I received information that thugs were looking for me in several refugee camps in Colombo and I was asked to hide in different places. By this time I had given up hope of leaving the country to attend the International Congress on Pastoral Care and Counselling that was to be held in San Francisco. However I was advised to make every effort to leave. After hiding in several places, my wife and I left our children with relatives and returned home to collect the things I would need for my journey.

It was certainly providential that I had been invited to the Congress in San Francisco and that the scholarship fund had sent my passage. I had, fortunately, booked my flight on Korean Airlines, which flies from Colombo every Saturday. And on August 4, I obtained a U.S. entry visa.

There was danger in my travelling from Colombo to the airport, but I had to risk it. Those who travel to the airport even in public transports are stopped and Tamils pulled out and attacked. Nevertheless, with the help of Sinhalese friends and high government officials who knew me and were able to accompany me to the airport in their private vehicles, I was able to "sneak out" of the country on Saturday, August 6, at night.

*   *   *

Discrimination: A Sinhalese Perspective

Much of the resentment of the Sinhalese majority stems from the time when the British plantation system was instituted, destroying local ag-

ricultures and bringing fears that the exploding Tamil population would compete for the few jobs available in the stagnant rural economy. The racial violence of recent years is an explosion of polarization that has been building for many generations.

Expatriate Tamils claim that the Tamil community in Sri Lanka is being discriminated against and that their only hope is to establish a separate state. We maintain that it is not a question of discrimination, but an attempt by the Tamils to retain the position of privilege they have enjoyed for several decades. Further, the expatriate Tamils claim that there are violations of human rights. We submit to you that the cry of human rights violations, while attracting world attention, is really a cover to maintain the status quo and to safeguard the vested interests of the Sri Lankan Tamils.

According to the 1981 census, Sri Lankan Tamils constitute 12.6 percent of the population. Of this number, one-third live among Sinhalese. Therefore only 8 percent of the population lives in the north. Yet the separatists demand nearly one-third of the area of Sri Lanka for a separate state.

During colonial times, education was mainly in the hands of missionaries. A strong missionary presence in the northern Tamil area, using more progressive forms of education in the applied sciences, gave Tamils a decided advantage regarding the professionals and government jobs. . . . Even though the national share of Tamil student population is on the order of 12 percent, . . . they represent 60 percent of the dental students, 40 percent of the medical students, 38 percent of the engineering students and 50 percent of the other undergraduates.

Health care facilities available to the Tamil community are superior to the average situation. . . for instance, there is one doctor per 9,500 persons on a national basis, whereas in the north [where most of the Tamils live] there is one doctor for every 7,000 persons.

Let us consider employment among Tamil professionals. According to 1982 figures: engineers: 35 percent; surveyors: 30 percent; doctors: 30 percent; vets: 40 percent; accountants: 32 percent. For 12 percent of the population to have such a high ration of employment in the professional fields cannot mean "discrimination". Unemployment is [also] decidedly lower among the Tamils than among Sinhalese.

If a people's quality of life, education faciles, and health care services reflect the rights and privileges accorded them, then Tamils in Sri Lanka have indeed been a decidedly privileged group. The human rights of the rest of the citizens of Sri Lanka to food, shelter, health care and education are being denied because the resources of the country are being diverted to counter terrorist activities of Tamils.

Excerpts from a speech given by a Sinhalese at a meeting of the National Council of the Churches of Christ in the U.S.A., February 1985.

FAITH
STREAMS

Introduction

All the major faiths of the world are alive and thriving in southern Asia. From Nepal, where the Buddha was born, to Pakistan, created as an Islamic nation, to India, home to most of the world's Hindus, Jains and Sikhs, streams of history, culture and tradition flow together to produce a unique religious context in which people live out their faith.

The stories in this section present a picture of the many faiths of southern Asia, but the common thread is the presence of Christ and Christianity. Without going into great depth on the long history of Christianity in southern Asia, consider the following points:

- the way the faith has influenced tribal peoples—for during British rule, the very current of tribal people's existence was dammed up. While Christians are a minority group throughout most of southern Asia it is important to note that in northeast India, Christians often make up a majority in the political fabric of certain states and here, tribal social structure has become the model for church organization.

- Jesus' disciple Thomas is believed to have been the founder of the Mar Thoma Orthodox Church, located mainly in the state of Kerala in south India. Thus while Christianity is often perceived by the Hindu majority to be a western faith, the Mar Thoma church is considered an indigenous Christian community rooted in the soil of India—not an implant from another culture.

- referring again to the minority status of Christians: according to 1982 statistics, in Bangladesh Christians make up .5 percent of the population; in Nepal, .05 percent; in India, 3.9 percent; in Sri Lanka, 9.1 percent.

- Most Christian communities in southern Asia, apart from the Mar Thoma church, have had difficulty discarding the western style that gives them an aura of "foreignness". And their minority status has not automatically brought Christians into positive, nurturing relationships with each other. But while divisions remain between Protestants, Catholics and Orthodox and between "evangelicals", "liberals", "conservatives" and "radicals", organic church union thrives in southern Asia.

NEPAL
The Story of Ganga Prasad Pradhan
by Jonathan Lindell

[In about 1870, in the early days of the Rana regime, there was a government servant who] worked in the kings' place at Hanuman Dhoka and had his home in Thamel Tole, Kathmandu. Upon the death of his wife, this husband and father made the radical decision to leave Nepal and seek a new life off to the east in Darjeeling, India.

After quitting his job and closing his affairs, the father took his 11-year-old son and started out over the main road into the eastern hills. This was a strange new world to them. They were town-bred . . . at home among the tight streets and bazaars of Kathmandu. Now they left the broad valley behind and rose to the ridge of mountains surrounding it. Crossing through the pass they found themselves looking at eye-level across an unbelievable jumble of mountains stretching off without end to the distant hazy horizon. Those who have been at sea have likened this view to that of the great swells and tossing waves of the ocean. The travellers stood aghast and wondered why they had left their home and what would happen to them if they took the plunge into that sea of mountains. But plunge they did, and three weeks later they came out at the other end, their city muscles hardened and their stomachs adjusted to mountain fare.

Arrival in India
One day the atmosphere changed, their step quickened with anticipation and coming up the hill they stopped on the border at small village called Simana. They were in British India.

[The father found a place to live in Bhutia Basti. Later, he established a small village there which is still known as Newar Gaon. After a while, he remarried and took employment as a contractor at Ging Tea Estate. With the entire family he moved to the estate and children were born to this new family.]

Ganga Prasad Pradhan is thought to be the first Nepali Christian. This account of his life is taken from the story as told by Jonathan Lindell in Nepal and the Gospel of God.

[The 11-year-old boy who had come from Nepal was active and precocious, picking up ideas and knowledge every day. Soon, people of the Church of Scotland Mission] opened a school near where he lived and he enrolled, giving his name as Ganga Prasad Pradhan. This name was to become famous throughout Darjeeling District and into literary circles in Nepal and even overseas. But now he was only a young lad attending a simple village school. To call it a simple village school was really to do it an injustice. It was, in fact, the most valuable single common possession of the village. Father Pradhan and his son had travelled through two hundred miles of eastern Nepal and very likely not seen a single village school. The idea of modern-type schools to educate the general public was not yet an idea in the minds of leadership in Nepal. It was an anti-establishment idea. There were [in Nepal] in communities of sufficient Brahmin population, small Sanskrit schools where Brahmin boys were taught the rudiments of their priestly language and the minimum needs for conducting the village paper business. The aristocracy of the country arranged for educating their own youth, either in Nepal or in India. But there was no idea in those days of general public education.

India was another story. It was booming. The Christian missions across the sub-continent were taking the lead and had opened schools by the hundreds.

Introduction to Christ

One of the books placed in the hands of students like Ganga Prasad was a small, thin book of thirty pages, bound with a thread and having a thin-papered red cover held on with glue. The name of this book was *School Questions and Answers*. From this book, Ganga Prasad and other students read their first lessons in Christian teachings.

By the time Ganga Prasad was reading in upper classes, the things about God were becoming alive in his mind and he thought seriously about sin and salvation. He got the little Bible book called "The Good News of the Lord Jesus Christ According to Luke" and read carefully in it. He started to pray to God and felt that God was close to him. Later, he began to talk to missionaries.

As his interest and faith in Christ grew he told his father about these new things, but his father strictly forbade him to follow them or become a Christian. As Ganga was coming into young [adulthood] his father died. This blow sent him more strongly into a consideration of the things of religion and he determined that now he could not only read and pray and learn, but that he could act and become a follower of Jesus Christ his Saviour. So he asked about how to become a Christian, and following advice from friends, he went away from the strict and forbidding environment of his home to Gaya, Bihar. There, among a group of Christians, he spoke about his faith in Christ and desire to be a disciple and was baptized.

[After more schooling in Ranchi, Bihar, Ganga Prasad] began to teach in a school and also to learn the job of printing in the small mission press. He grew in maturity, in knowledge, in skills. He became respected as a leader among Christians and a guide to others to belief in Jesus Christ.

[As the message of the Gospel was received, one of the growing needs was for literature. Ganga Prasad wrote some of the needed books, opened his own printing press and went into the printing business.] For twenty-five years he was the co-partner with a turnover of three Scottish missionaries in translating first the whole New Testament and the whole Old Testament into Nepali.

Nepali Christians Desire to Share Their Faith

These Nepalese in India were one of the multiplying groups in villages on the border who began to preach and teach with the hope and desire that someday they might go and live in their own country. They sent a petition to the [Nepali] government with such a request, but never received a reply.

Ganga Prasad was one who longed to return to his people to share the Good News. Joined by his son-in-law and others, [he and] a group of about forty Nepalese Christians gave up their good jobs, packed up their earthly possessions and set off to return. The trip was arduous but their spirits were high and even the loss of most of their possessions by thieves did not dampen their spirits. During the three-week wait at the border for permission to enter, a number of the original forty returned to Darjeeling. When permission was granted, the rest of the group set forth with great anticipation.

They spent their first days in Kathmandu searching for a home to rent. Upon visiting the King, Maharja Chandra, and requesting permission to reside in the country, they were told no Christians could live in the kingdom and he instructed them to return to India. So, escorted by two soldiers, they found themselves ushered to the border and eventually found their way back to Darjeeling and Kalimpong. These people had sought and found something and were telling about it, but Nepal would have nothing of it.

Editor's note: There is a Nepali church in Nepal, but it is under pressure from a government that continues to proclaim that Nepali Christians have no place in Nepal. For the protection of the faithful, there is limited reference made to the current Christian fellowship in Nepal. See page 51 for one story of faith and courage in Nepal.

The United Mission to Nepal

A unique form of missional partnership exists for the Christian presence and witness in Nepal. Since the relaxation of some of the restrictions on foreign presence in Nepal "in 1951, some Christians have come into the country and are working with government aid missions, in government posts, schools and projects. Some of these Christians are Indians and a good number of them are Nepali by race and language.

"Wherever these Christians are located they naturally form themselves into small groups or congregations for fellowship and encouragement. If the size of the group merits it, they arrange for a pastor, administer the sacraments and in a few cases have put up buildings or 'places of worship.'

"The National Law of 1963 allows people to remain in the religion of their forefathers, protects them from pressures to convert to other religions and defines penalties where this law is broken. With 'proselytizing' thus forbidden, the United Mission to Nepal does not pastor congregations nor baptize people. It has no organizational connection with congregations which have grown up quite independently of foreign interference or control. Workers in the UMN, however, do enjoy fellowship with other Christians, both expatriate and Nepali, and join in as individuals (not as a Mission) with . . . Christians in the worship life and witness of the groups and congregations where they live."

As the UMN developed it did so in full agreement with the government. It did not go its independent private way. It is interesting to note that the original agreement, called the "Dikshit letter", written in 1953, had four simple terms; the latest one, written in 1975, has sixteen terms of agreement. Some of the terms are:

1) The Mission should give medicine to patients without cost—in other words, do its medical work more or less for free;

2) The Mission is responsible for the financial construction and running of the projects which it establishes—in other words, without financial assistance from the Government;

Barbara H. Chase quotes from "Nepal (and the UMN) at a Glance", a 1984 United Mission to Nepal publication, and from Jonathan Lindell's **Nepal and the Gospel of God.**

3) Mission members shall be subject to the laws of the land;

4) "No person shall propagate Christianity, Islam or any other faith so as to disrupt the traditional religion of the Hindu community within Nepal, or convert any adherent of the Hindu religion into these faiths."

"The term in the Agreement which restricts converting and the term allowing many forms of service both have sent the Mission into deep study of the New Testament to understand better just what the Lord assigns it to do in the place where it is. Certain passages have become especially illuminating and personally instructive , such as:

Peace be with you. As the Father has sent me, even so I send you. (John 20:21)

Whatever you do, in word or deed, do everything in the name of the Lord Jesus. (Col.3:17) [This is also in the UMN Constitution]

"The clauses limiting the time that the Mission may be in Nepal certainly have been influential in the attitudes and planning of the Mission. It realizes that its presence is temporary and it tries to be ready to move on. . . .

"Little by little, over many days stretching into years, the Mission has learned lessons of attitudes, status and relationships so that its people have come to work in faith and joy in a warm association."

Working in the Hindu Kingdom of Nepal the UMN workers have gained appreciation for the leaders of the country so that it is truly a partnership with His Majesty's government and also with Nepali society.

PAKISTAN
To Be a Christian in an Islamic Country
by Bishop Michael J. Nasir Ali

In this chapter Bishop Nasir Ali addresses the issues of "contextualization" and "inculturation." "Contextualization" refers to what happens when the church takes serious account of the place in which it is located and the political, economic and social realities of that context. The church must also be deeply involved in and share the culture of the people it serves— that is, it must engage in "inculturation". In Pakistan this has unique implications, for to be Pakistani, for the majority of the population, means to be Muslim. To be Pakistani and Christian is to be forced to ask how one can be a faithful Christian and yet also be part of the Islamic culture. To speak out on "inculturation" and "contextualization" is somewhat radical for a Pakistani priest. For one thing, many Pakistani Christians originally came from India and are still attached to their Hindu cultural background. There are also those in Pakistan who are attracted to Christianity largely because of its western cultural aura. How, then, to live in an officially Islamic country as a faithful Christian?

In the context of Islam, [contextualization or inculturation] is a cylical problem, i.e.: How much is there in Islam which was taken directly or indirectly from Christian sources? The influence of Christian monasticism on Sufism and the influence of the later fathers on the development of *kalam*, or formal theology in Islam, is well established. It is also known that many of the early mosques had been Christian churches, and the influence of oriental Christianity is readily apparent in Muslim architecture. If, therefore, Christians in a Muslim context decide to build churches that look like mosques they are only reappropriating something they have given Islam.

There are many other areas of influence. The witness of the ancient churches in Islamic lands is particularly valuable in this

At a 1983 consultation on evangelism, Bishop Michael J. Nasir Ali of the Raiwind Diocese of the Church of Pakistan presented a paper titled, "Evangelization in an Islamic Context: A Profile", from which this chapter is taken.

context. As we have seen, there was a great deal that Islam borrowed from them, but they adapted as well. This adaptation was at several levels:

Social and cultural: [Christians] learned to live as a politically powerless minority which, nevertheless, wielded great influence culturally and commercially. In matters of social etiquette they made every effort to adjust. Sometimes, of course, they had no choice in the matter. The dress of the Coptic clergy [in Egypt], for example, was regulated by the state and continues to be, even today! They adopted the language of the rulers (Arabic) for day-to-day social intercourse, although they kept their own ecclesiastical and liturgical languages alive as well.

Theological and liturgical: Eventually, [Christians in ancient churches] adopted *"Allah"* [the Islamic expression for God] as their usual word for God, though there had been some early polemic against it. When the Bible came to be translated into Arabic, *Allah* was used as the word for God. In the translations of the liturgies, too, *Allah* is often used. Many of their characteristics of worship, such as attitudes of reverence and the wealth of symbolic language in the liturgies are, in any case, consonant with Muslim culture. So are socio-liturgical practices, such as the segregation of the sexes during divine worship. The early church rejected the practice of excluding women from the body of the synagogue, but retained segregation of the sexes. The ancient churches continue this practice to a large extent.

Despite adaptation, the ancient churches maintain a vigorous counter-culture which witnesses to Gospel values.

Contextualization in Pakistan Today

Culturally, at least, the Punjabi church is well-integrated into the community; Punjabi Christians speak the same language, have the same lifestyle and the same problems as their Muslim Punjabi brethren. Some problems, however, remain. These include the kind of "petty apartheid" which operates against poorer Christians because some of them are sweepers. This is a Hindu hangover in Muslim Pakistan. In Islam, of course, there is no caste consciousness, but sweeping is regarded as an unclean profession among caste Hindus.

As far as worship is concerned, the Punjabi psalms are well contextualized and non-Christians admire their language and the classical *raags* (music) to which they are usually set.

The language of the liturgies is getting increasingly contextualized. In some churches, for example, the Gospel is now sung in the way the Qu'ran [the holy book of Islam] is chanted. (The cylical nature of contextualization in an Islamic context is illustrated here; [for] the chanting of the Qu'ran was borrowed from the singing of the lections in the Syrian Christian liturgies. Indeed, the word

"Qu'ran" itself is related to the Syriac *Queryana*, which means the Scripture reading!)

Before we proceed, however, it is best to highlight a problem which Christians in Pakistan are facing today: Should contextualization take place with reference to folk-culture or with reference to orthodox Islam? A case in point is the development of indigenous Christian music and its use in worship. In orthodox Islam, the use of musical instruments in worship is forbidden, although such instruments are widely used in *qawwali* (a popular folk-devotion). In Christian worship, however, indigenous musical instruments are widely used and, indeed, many of the forms of indigenous Christian music have been borrowed from *qawwali*. Contextualization has occured here at the level of folk-culture. The problem is being experienced in a sharper way in the south, where many tribal Hindus are becoming Christians. The church is busy contextualizing the worship of these new Christians according to their Hindu folk-culture. Thus a great many *bhajans* (these are songs which narrate the events of the Gospels in the way the Hindus narrate the events of the Hindu epics) are being produced. Again, at weddings, instead of going around the fire as was their previous (Hindu) custom, Christian couples walk around the cross. The problem is that ultimately, these Christians will have to come to terms with Pakistani culture, which is, of course, Muslim culture. How far then should contextualization into the Hindu context be encouraged?

The Other Side of Contextualization

Without touching on the problem of syncretism, which may become a problem, there are areas of difficulty as far as contextualization is concerned. There is, for example, in our context, the uncritical acceptance of the Muslim worldview. Then there is the subconscious acceptance of the Muslim theory of revelation and its application (or misapplication) to the Christian scriptures. This has caused many problems in Pakistan, sometimes even resulting in schism. At times there is a *conscious* desire to imitate as, for instance, the attempt by certain Christians to provide an alternative "Christian" system equivalent to the Muslim *shari'at* (law). At the popular level, too, there is imitation, as in the adoption of *purdah* (wearing of the veil) by Christian women when they achieve a certain socio-economic status. On occasion, attempts are made to "Christianize" superstitions. An example of this is the way the consecrated elements are sometimes used to prepare amulets. At the level of worship, too, there seem to be undesirable influences, such as the tendency to preach repetitive exhortatory sermons at the expense of expository ones and the increasing use of loudspeakers fixed outside the churches.

A historical perspective of Christian attempts at contextualization compels us to ask certain questions about the process. First, how much diversity is permissible? In other words, what minimum uniformity should there be? The early church permitted a great deal of cultural adaptation, but scripture, the dominical sacraments and the unity and mutual recognition of ministries set limits to what was permissible. It is possible to imagine a church today which has a "dynamic equivalence" translation of the Bible, contextualized sacraments (yoghurt and *nan*, a kind of bread, in one local instance) and a radical view of ministry. So far so good, but the question remains as to what continuity such a church would have with the church through the ages and around the world? Should there be a distinctive Christian counterculture in a given society, or should Christians integrate as much as possible?

In other words, should we be a light, clearly seen but separate, or should we be as salt or leaven, changing society from the inside? Perhaps these two models are not mutually exclusive. The ancient churches in Islamic lands, at any rate, have managed both to retain and to develop their own counterculture and to influence their society at large in the fields of education, commerce and even politics.

SRI LANKA
"Liberation" According to the Buddha and Christ
by Dr. Antony Fernando

Buddha's atheism and Christ's theism are not two attitudes that are antagonistic to each other. Both have one common aim: to awaken people to a sense of realism and responsibility in their day-to-day life.

We have to go a step further and inquire if Christ understood religion and liberation exactly as the Buddha did; in other words, if the main concern of Christ, too, was the transformation of the inner personality of humankind . . .

In the search for the right answer, a Christian here is bound to meet with a preliminary difficulty. The word "liberation" does not figure so prominently in the language of Christ as in that of the Buddha. What [Jesus] used by preference is the term "Kingdom of Heaven". It is that term that a Christian student will have to explore to find out if Buddha's notion of liberation was common to Christ too . . . . If that barrier caused by the distance of time can be overcome . . . we will automatically be led to conclude that the "Kingdom" of Christ is not very different from the *nirvana* of Buddha.

That abrupt statement, of course, could cause a certain dismay to someone who hears it for the first time. The identification or even the approximation of *nirvana* with the Kingdom could shock as much the Buddhist as the Christian.

That is because they are terms that are very sacred to both. *Nirvana* and the Kingdom represent for the Buddhist and the Christian, respectively, the ultimate life-goal that each has to aspire to in his [or her] own special way. Therefore the Buddhist and the Christian cannot be blamed if each considers [this ultimate] goal so unique as to resent it being compared to another's.

But in the original usage of the Buddha and Christ, *nirvana* and

---

Dr. Antony Fernando is lecturer in Christian Culture at the University of Kelaniya in Sri Lanka. This selection is taken from his book, Buddhism and Christianity—Their Inner Affinity, *(Colombo: Ecumenical Institute for Study and Dialogue, 1981).*

the Kingdom are realities that pertain primarily to an individual's life on earth. They designate the fullness of the humanhood that an individual could achieve here and how.

An analytical study of [their] teachings would show without any trace of doubt that the main aim of Christ's ministry was the same as that of Buddha, namely the uplifting of an individual's inner personality. If that fact can be definitely established then there would be no gainsaying the fact that, with regard to the notion of liberation, there is a great affinity in the thought of Buddha and Christ.

If the imagery of Christ can be correctly understood, . . . [his] love-of-neighbor stories will be seen to teach one simple lesson: [that] humankind essentially is a related being. If truly human, life must express that relatedness or neighborliness. Charity is not just a meritorious action that one is free to do or not to do. Only a person concerned about others deserves to be called a human being, a religious person.

[This teaching], as anyone would readily grant, is not exclusive to Christianity. It is found in Buddhism too. Lovingkindness, or *maitriya* (literally, friendliness), is for the Buddha an indispensable characteristic of the adult human being.

The [Christian] doctrines of providence and forgiveness, of course, are not found in that identical form in Buddhism. But it is not impossible that the sense of realism they represent is contained altogether in a different shape in Buddhism too. Buddha's teaching on "no-self" (*annata*), for example, is deep enough to embrace the message underlying even those doctrines.

For both [Christ and the Buddha], the field of operation was exactly the same: the mind of humankind. It was the mind of humankind that was sick. It was the mind of humankind that had to be cured. Humankind's mind was blank and had to be cured by being awakened to a realistic view of life.

It is that singlemindedness of the Buddha and Christ with regard to the aim of religion that would lead anyone to conclude that there is a strong inner affinity between Buddhism and Christianity. Even the fact that Christianity is theistic and Buddhism non-theistic does not minimize in any way that unity of vision that both the Buddha and Christ had with regard to the nature of religion and its primary function.

INDIA
Christ in Indian Thought: A Dialogue

When we look at the Christian faith in southern Asia we must realize that it exists alongside other living faiths—a reality with which western Christianity has not had to wrestle until recently. The following imaginary dialogue includes outstanding theologians, scholars and poets of different faiths who lived in India in both the 19th and 20th centuries. Time has been condensed to allow them to explore together the history and current reality of Christianity in their own settings. The participants are:

V. Chakkarai, one of the creative thinkers of the "rethinking Christianity group" of the late 1930's;

Mohandas K. Gandhi, father of independent India, founder of the doctrine of nonviolence to achieve political and social progress;

Sarvepalli Radhakrishnan, Hindu scholar and president of India from 1962 to 1967. From 1946 to 1952 he led the Indian delegation to UNESCO;

Rabindranath Tagore, Bengali author and poet, Nobel laureate in 1913, and scion of the Brahmo Samaj, a Hindu reform movement;

P.D. Sham Rao, Director of the Christian Retreat and Study Center in Rajpur;

Richard W. Taylor, one of the first staff members of the Christian Institute for the Study of Religion and Society, with headquarters in Bangalore. Dr. Taylor is based in New Delhi.

D.A. Thangasamy, principal of St. John's College in Palayamkottai;

M.M. Thomas, chief social theologian and founding associate director of the Christian Institute for the Study of Religion and Society, he became its director and is now director *emeritus*.

This "dialogue", conceived and edited by Martha L. Man, *uses material from the writings of Chakkarai, Gandhi, Radhakrishnan, Tagore, Sham Rao , Richard W. Taylor, Thangasamy and M.M. Thomas. Sources are listed under "Notes", page 95.*

The Dialogue Begins

Richard W. Taylor: Since the beginning of the nineteenth century, most Indian Christian theological thinking has been done by people who were not professional theologians. Some of the most stimulating bits of it have been done by people who never themselves became Christian. Most of it is Christological—it is about Jesus Christ rather than about God or the Holy Spirit. In India I think that this is both because Jesus and his teachings have been so attractive and because talking about him is specifically Christian, whereas talking about God in this land of many gods or talking about the Spirit in this land of many spirits may be rather less clear than it would be in some other places.[1]

Sarvepalli Radhakrishnan: What you think of Christ is undoubtedly a most important problem. To an educated Hindu, Jesus is a supreme illustration of the growth from human origins to divine destiny. As a mystic who believes in the inner light, Jesus ignores ritual and is indifferent to legalistic piety. He is contemptuous of the righteousness of the scribes and the Pharisees. Being otherworldly in spirit, he is indifferent to the wealth of the world and exalts poverty as one of the greatest goods. He wishes us to restrain not only our outward actions but our inner desires and to carry the principle of non-attachment even into the sphere of family relationships. He is the great hero who exemplifies the noblest characteristics of manhood [sic.], the revealer of the profoundest depths in ourselves, one who brings home to us the ideal of human perfection by embodying it visibly in himself . . . For me, the person of Jesus is a historical fact. Christ is not a datum of history but a judgement of history. Jesus' insight is expressive of a timeless spiritual fact; but what the theologians say of it are afterthoughts, interpretations of the fact, *viz.*, the life and death of Jesus.[2]

M.M. Thomas: Christology is central to Christian theology. Every symbol, every sacrament, every doctrine in Christianity points to the simple assertion that Jesus is the Christ. Christian dialogue with the secular world and with [those] of other faiths is a dialogue about Christ. Christian apologetics is oriented to the assertion that God was in Christ reconciling the world to Himself.[3]

Granted this centrality of Jesus Christ, there is no limit to the possibility of integrating into Christian spirituality elements of the spirituality of other faiths, elements which express the unknown or the partially-acknowledged Christ. There is a fundamental difference, however, between mixing and integrating. The former is incoherent and revolves around many centers and has, in the long run, a disintegrating effect. The latter is a unity with one center, Jesus Christ. In acknowledging His lordship over human existence and His eternal sonship of the Father and unity with the Holy Spirit, every spirituality goes through the crisis of death to be renewed and integrated in Christ.[4]

Taylor: Some of the leaders of the Brahmo Samaj, a Hindu reform movement, had a great deal to say about Jesus and some remarkable Indian ways of seeing Him.[5] Notable among these were Ram Mohan Roy, the founder of the Brahmo Samaj, sometimes called the Father of Modern India, who wrote *The Precepts of Jesus,* and Keshab Chandra Sen, . . . who lectured and published extensively on Christ. Both were in close touch with Unitarians throughout the English-speaking world. Rabindranath Tagore, you also have written and spoken extensively about the humanity of Jesus, haven't you?[6]

Rabindranath Tagore: The Son of Man . . . touched the untouchable, he ate with the outcasts and instead of rejecting the sinners he beckoned them to the way of salvation . . . He called his disciples and said, "he who clothes those without clothes, clothes me." Service to humanity is the worship of those who take Christ's teaching seriously . . . By Jesus' advent God's love has been revealed to all. Who has preached the greatness of humanity as Jesus Christ has? His disciples called him a Man of Sorrow. Jesus accepted sorrow in a great way and thereby has made humankind great. When an individual makes himself known on the basis of suffering, then he announces his undiluted humanity which cannot be quenched by fire or rent by weapons. [Such a person] has preached the love of God through the love of all humankind. So it is not surprising that Jesus should take upon himself voluntarily the suffering of all. It is the religion of love to come forward and bear the burden of sorrow voluntarily and vicariously . . . The love that has life gains glory by self-sacrifice, by affirming suffering.[7]

Taylor: Tagore, you also spoke of Jesus as *Mahapurush. Maha* [in Sanskrit] means big or great. (It is the same word that is combined with *atma,* meaning soul, to give the title *Mahatma*—great soul— to M.K. Gandhi.) *Purush* means man, "male person", but not so much mere "man", as "primal man". Toward the end of the *Rig-Veda, purusha* becomes one of the most important entities. His sacrificial death giving rise to the multiplicity of creation is described in detail in this Hindu scripture. The Brahmo Samaj sought to purify Hinduism by dropping late distortions in order to return to the purity of the vedas. It seems to be highly significant that you, Tagore, should select *purusha* from the final development of the fundamental veda, the *Rig-Veda,* as the basis for your final treatment of Jesus—Jesus as *Mahapurush.*[8]

Tagore: Yes, by sacrificing, this *Mahapurush* has reached the door of death and brought the message of love. Because of this, Jesus opened the supreme path by being born in a poor home. His followers did not understand his message . . . they were overwhelmed. This message was not pursued only by the Christians. Many in the history of the world have rejected his message. They are the people who have crucified the Christ again and again.

Christianity has raised the dignity of human beings. When I can sacrifice in the name of truth, when I can say "brother and sister" with undiluted love, that day the son of the Father will be born in me. That would be our Christmas. Even today, Jesus Christ is being crucified every day through greed and war perpetrated and perpetuated by the western nations. He called all people children of the heavenly Father. Jesus said they should be reconciled with each other . . . [and] sacrificed his life at the alter of humanity.[9]

Thomas: The purpose of Indian interpretations of Christ is not to create an Indian theology as such, but to communicate the message of the Christ. This is to say that the intention of the writers of the New Testament as to the reality of Christ is to be "translated" in Indian language, idiom and symbolism. . . . Here at the very outset one is overwhelmed with the complexity of the Indian religious tradition, albeit differing in various regions of India. There is, therefore, the need for a pluralism in Christology to see the diverse needs of the situation. We must think in terms of Christologies rather than a Christology. Each type will have its own apologetic problems . . .

The Indian religious tradition is more prone to emphasize the divinity of Jesus at the cost of his humanity. But a Christ devoid of his human nature would not be the Christ. He would be a God walking on earth, an *avatara,* a divine being in the vestments of a human. He would not "resemble [humankind] in every respect." He would be less than wholly relevant for the salvation of all people. It is "because he himself has suffered and been tempted, he is able to help those who are tempted." (Heb. 2:18)[10]

Chakkarai, don't you see the uniqueness of Jesus Christ in the abiding presence of Christ, rather than in the rejection of Hinduism?

V. Chakkarai: In the Christian as well as in the Indian religious experience, the incarnation took time to assume a certain doctrinal rigidity. But the real feature to be noted is this: that whereas the Indian incarnations, for instance Rama and Krishna, were temporary and passed away, the Christian view that we are describing is that it is abiding and permanent. The Spirit of Jesus is incarnated again and again in human hearts, and to use language that the New Testament has made familiar to us, God dwells with [human beings] and his tabernacle is among the children of [human beings], not merely by their side, but in them. Rama and Krishna passed away from the world after having done their respective duties, the one through plunging into a river and the other killed by a hunter. There is no promise and certainly no consciousness that their spirits would come back and abide with human spirits. In the case of Jesus this is evidently different; the earliest Christian experience and the available documentary evidence, removed from the death of our Lord by only fifteen years, are alike confirmatory.[11]

Taylor: A lone Catholic voice for much of his life was Brahmo-bandhab Upadhayaya, who was with Rabindranath Tagore at Saniniketan for while in the early twentieth century. Upadhayaya advocated living in a Hindu caste lifestyle and did it so thoroughly that for most of the last years of his life he was thought to have forsaken Christianity.[12]

Thomas: The assertion that there is salvation in no one else, for there is no other name under heaven given among all people by which we must be saved (Acts 4:12), has been the subject of real debate. The Hindus have found it unacceptable and the main burden of Christian theology in India has been to communicate the message of the crucified and risen Lord, the only name to which every knee should bow on earth and in heaven.[13]

D.A. Thangasamy: . . . the traditional Hindu view—which, however, is perceptibly changing as Hindu swamis take to evangelistic missions and set up centers of Hindu worship and teaching abroad—[is that] there is no need for conversation from one religion to another because, as V.A. Devasenapathi has noted, "sincere efforts to reach the goal along the path pursued by one's predecessors will bring success sooner or later."[14]

Gandhi: I could no more think of asking a Christian or a Muslim or a Parsi to change his [or her] faith than I would think of changing my own.[15]

Taylor: The "rethinking Christianity" group included some of the most creative thinkers in the history of Indian Christian theology. . . . They sought to set Indian Christianity right in the center of Indian culture and ideas and society. They were doubtful about the usefulness and relevance of the received western theology. They were much more doubtful about the relevance of received institutional church structures. They thought patterns of life and association derived from an understanding of the Kingdom of God to be much better and more important than the received patterns of church structure.[16]

P.D. Sham Rao: The uniqueness of Christ as preached by the church does not go unquestioned. Many in India claim that Jesus was influenced by the Buddhistic thought. A sect among the Muslims claim that he had visited India and died here. The church's lifestyle which is not consistent with its preaching is heavily criticized. One of the prominent Indian thinkers has said that Christians are ordinary people with extraordinary claims. Christianity is no more considered "the way", but one of the many ways that leads humankind to salvation.[17]

Taylor: From the 1920's, most creative Protestant thinking was related to or permeated by Indian nationalism. This made it especially threatening to the churches, all of which, on the whole, owed loyalty to the colonial state—this was largely because they were still led by missionaries who either supported the colonial state out of conviction or were in India on visas which required their loyalty.[18]

Rao: Different faiths and ideologies and religious sects are deeply convinced that their way of life and their ideology is the answer to the problems of the world. They not only hold this conviction but present it to the world as the only way or the best way among the rest. Followers of Arya Samaj have been systematically working to convert back to the fold of Hinduism all those who had accepted Christianity.[19]

Taylor: Neither the monks who founded the Catholic ashram movement, nor the large number of sensitive and pioneering people who followed them into it, nor the South Asian critics of it, seem to realize that an essential of the mainstream of modern Indian ashrams involved the promotion of rather radical social, economic and political change.[20]

Rao: Most of the time, the church is not aware that through its preaching it is answering a question which the Indian situation has not asked. . . . What is needed is to discern the question which the people in a given situation are asking about their existence, and then present Christ as the answer to that particular question . . . [Each] situation demands that Christ be presented as the answer to their problem of being victimized by the existential anxiety of fate and death.[21]

D. A. Thangasamy: The Christian Gospel, like communism, will not be contained within boundaries of country or race or language [or sex]. It is good news to be broadcast to every corner of the world and it must bring about changes in the behavior and the ways of life of people who respond to it. But some of the changes may be embarrassing to those who accept the good news and exasperating to those who regard it as deplorable. Hence the controversies regarding conversion right from the first.[22]

I believe that God is teaching us that it takes many races, ways of worship and experiences of mind and spirit to make the Universal Church, and that perceptions of truth which appear to be contradictory may really be complementary. For a long time now we have pondered the need for unity in ecumenism. Perhaps we should now turn to explore the meaning of ecumenism in terms of diversity.[23]

BANGLADESH
The Church Today in Bangladesh

Christian communities in Bangladesh were recognized as legitimate after the 1971 war of liberation when they started an all-out relief and rehabilitation program for all people. When secularism—the separation of church and state—was adopted as one of the four principles on which the new nation of Bangladesh was to be built, it became possible for the Christian churches to "indigenize" their life and witness. Since Christians had been part of the struggle for liberation, had fought alongside Muslim men and women, many had hoped that a bond of understanding would be forged. But when secularism was replaced by a commitment to *shari'at* (Islamic law), the churches found themselves on the defensive again. Today, some segments of the Christian community are engaged in an examination of their history and their role in society.[1]

Why Has the Growth of Christianity Been So Slow?
Statistics indicate that the Christian community grew from .09 percent of the population in 1891 to .28 percent in 1974. It is suggested that one reason for this slow growth is that both Islam and Hinduism are deeply rooted in the history and soil of Bangladesh. Christianity is identified with the West and with imperialism, and Bangladeshis have been slow to accept this foreign faith.

Because of this attitude, Christian missions concentrated on education, social services and medical care, and later on social action. In 1974, Bangladesh had the lowest percentage of Christian missionaries in both the Protestant and Roman Catholic communities of any country open to such missions.

The Roman Catholic church has identified the following as barriers which have reduced the church's relevance to Islamic society: (1) lack of dialogue with Muslims; (2) the impossibility of conversion for Muslims; (3) identification of the church as a relief agency; (4) the church's non-identification with Bengali culture; (5) the use

Written by Barbara H. Chase from background resources on Bangladesh listed under "Notes", page 96.

of traditional foreign church liturgy which is foreign to Bengali culture; (6) over-representation of foreign personnel; and (7) the lack of trained leaders.[2]

What Approach to Mission is Needed?

Bishop Labayan of the Roman Catholic Church in the Philippines points out that the role of the church is that of a witness demonstrating to all the Gospel values. Then non-Christians, seeing the possibilities that lie within each person, might be inspired to act according to these values—but not necessarily by becoming Christian! From this perspective, interreligious and intercultural dialogue should be the principal means of preaching the Gospel while at the same time rendering service to the weakest members of society. In other words, serving Bangladeshis with no ulterior motive of converting them.[3]

The church being part of the culture of the people it serves is a way in which the gospel is spread. What has happened in Bangladesh is that the Christian's lifestyle and culture are dominated by *Hindu* tradition and reflect little of *Bengali* culture. So the question arises: how can the church accept and be part of the culture in a country with a predominantly Islamic culture?   Dialogue with Muslims is in its infancy; it does not seem to be high on the priority list of any church. But for the church to be rooted in the soil of this Islamic nation it must find a way towards creative dialogue. The church needs to start its dialogue with Muslims from points of commonality, sharing common goals for the betterment of society.

[Islam] is a significant force in Bangladesh. It united East and West Pakistan in their struggle against India. It justified the liberation war (and was used as a cover for many of the atrocities). It influenced world powers in their formulation of policies towards the subcontinent. Islam is the moral rationale behind the aid given to fellow-Muslims, [such as] the the Rohingyas, a Muslim minority group of Arkan that sought refuge in Bangladesh after allegedly having been victimized by the Burmese. Islam serves as the *raison d'être* of looking for help from the OPEC countries. It is behind the trend of Bangladeshis finding employment in the Middle East. For Muslims, Islam provides a frame of reference, prescribing all behavioral norms and sanctions. It continuously reaffirms a Muslims's identity and distinguishes him or her from any other religious group. In Bangladesh, Christians are not only a numerical minority group but are seen as aliens; they must try to discover their place in the Muslim community while searching for ways to be real witnesses to the Christ they follow.[4]

WOMEN: CURRENTS OF CHANGE

Introduction

One wonders how both India and Sri Lanka could be among the first countries in the modern world to have women as prime ministers, yet allow most of the women in these countries to remain mired in social oppression, as expressed in the poem from India and the report from Sri Lanka in this section. The chapter on Bangladesh describes how social changes cannot be implemented until women's attitudes about themselves are transformed. And while the chapter on Pakistan shows how Islamic laws devalue women, women of all faiths have joined together to protest them and be heard. From Nepal comes a story of one woman's courageous witness in a country where Christian faith cannot be openly expressed. As Joyotsan Chatterji, a Christian writer from India, knows: "A woman is never an end in herself. She is the center of a pool whose ripples will reach out to all the farthest banks. Thus in reaching out to women we reach out to all persons."*

*Jyotsna Chatterji, ed. *Women in Praise and Struggle,* (New Delhi, ISPCK, 1982). Published for WCSRC-CISRS Joint Women's Progam and William Carey Study and Research Center, pp. 67, 68.

INDIA
LET US SAY
by Aruna Gnanadason

They say . . .
Stop climbing trees, you are a big girl now
Wear a saree, bangles, necklace and earrings too
It's dark, get home soon, it can be dangerous for you
Get educated—but we tell you where and why and what
This is because we will have to see that you find a suitable man
You want to study more . . . no, we think that is enough.

They say . . .
He has come
Quick, bedeck yourself like a neon light
Walk demurely, head bent down, in front of ogling, learning eyes
Smile gently, talk softly, sing a song, dance a dance
Play the veena, do not sneeze, do a rangeli design
Impress them, just impress them, don't let us down now
Don't sigh, if he weighs you against pieces of gold
Don't cry, if he bargains over you as if you were a cow to be sold
Don't sorrow, if he rejects you, someone else may come along
You are chosen at last, he's a good catch, you are very lucky, you
    know.

They say . . .
Your body is your womb, be fruitful and multiply
Don't cry out aloud, have you no shame, learn self control
A woman can bear pain, can adjust, can succumb to all insults

---

Aruna Gnanadason is executive secretary of the All-India Council of Christian Women of the Sub-unit of Women of the National Council of Churches in India.

Your home is your temple, your husband your lord
Be a good daughter-in-law, obey everyone, the system must go on
The story of women's oppression does not end here, my friend
On the other side it continues, read on and comprehend.

They say . . .
You must go out to work, how will the economy survive
But don't ask for more wages, that's all we will give
Don't blame us if you are sexually exploited, learn to fend for
    yourself
Sorry we have to fire you, there's a machine to do your job
Don't join the worker's union, that's for others not for you
Don't get involved in dirty politics, that's unfeminine too
Don't think of the plight of your underprivileged and *dalit*
    sisters
You have so much work to do.

They say . . .
Your body is not yours, it is for us to decide
To burn, if the dowry you came with is not enough
To rape, if a lesson must be taught to your man
To advertise, if the goods produced have to be sold
To control, if we feel that two children are all you must have
To sell, if the lust of man is to be satisfied
To starve, if there is not enough food for everyone
To exploit as cheap labor, doing peripheral jobs
We will decide, do not interfere, just leave everything to us.

They say, they say, they say . . .
Can we leave everything to them
The capitalists, the landlords, the exploiting classes and castes
Who control and enslave the majority—both men and women?
Come sisters, let us break out of our shackles
We have nothing to lose but our chains
Let us tear out of our double oppression
Our bodies are our own
Let us arise and unite women
Form unions, take up causes, assert our rights
Let our song of liberation encompass all who are oppressed
Let us shout aloud, let us cry out
Let our silent voices now be heard
Now is the time for us to say
Now is the time for us to decide
Come, sisters come, let us say, let us decide!

BANGLADESH
Half the Population in Bondage
by Joysree Baroi

An English reporter, in an article on Bangladesh, called the women of the country "the most unfortunate women in the world." I am not in a position to make comparisons as I have been nothing but a Bengali woman all my life. But certain incidents which I have seen, heard or read about during these years have helped to bring the male-female relationship in Bangladesh into perspective for me.

When I was in school (I was no more than twelve or thirteen years old at the time) I read a newspaper report which stated that an eleven-year-old bride had been murdered by her husband and mother-in-law. They had poured kerosene over her and set her alight because her father had failed to give the dowry he had promised at the time of marriage. I have never been able to forget that incident as it represents a part of my growing up. I began to realize slowly that girls are somehow different from boys, not very desirable as offspring because they represent a drain on the resources of their parents and are certainly not an asset since they can rarely work outside the home and earn money.

Education for Women
Women who have had the chance of getting an education are fortunate in that they have a greater say in their homes and they can, if their parents or husbands are agreeable, hold a job. The fact that I am speaking here today indicates that I belong to that privileged minority. Education gives the power to articulate but does not necessarily liberate, since the very system of education is designed to make people conform. For the woman who wishes to

---

Joysree Baroi was a postgraduate physics student at the University of Dhaka, Bangladesh when she gave this address at the 1977 Assembly of the Christian Conference of Asia, held in Penang, Malaysia. Her story was originally published in the assembly report, Testimony Amid Asian Suffering.

44

break free from the mold it is a long and lonely battle and most of us give up in the end.

What Hope for the Illiterate?

For those who are illiterate, the situation is very much worse. The majority of our women will not appear in front of strangers, much less talk to them. Society sees to it that a woman's inferior position is obvious to all. She walks behind her husband and takes her meals after him. The men of the house always eat first, then the children, and lastly, the women. Quite often, there is little rice and curry left when it is the wife's turn to eat. If she does not feel like cooking again—which happens quite frequently, since she is probably worn out by this time—she makes do with what is left. What happens if she is expecting a child? The situation does not change; she still cannot eat before her husband has eaten. The best of the food—the choicest cuts of meat and fish, the best vegetables, etc.—goes to him. The needs of pregnant and nursing women are ignored. This is perhaps a factor contributing to the comparatively high mortality rate of women of child-bearing age in our country. Another is the high death rate of infants, which compels parents to seek more children, thus adversely affecting the health of the women. The number of deaths of females in the fifteen to twenty-four age group exceeds the male mortality rate of the same age group by a ratio of seven to four.

The Meaning of Children for Women

It is these children, however, who give a Bangladeshi woman a sense of identity. After a child's birth, she is considered to have fulfilled her duty as a woman and is known from then on as her offspring's mother; for example she is called "Malek's mother" by everybody and not Rahima if that is her name. If she gives birth to girls only, it is considered a great misfortune and she has to suffer agonies of embarrassment in silence when people exclaim what a pity it is that she does not have any sons. For the childless woman, life takes on a nightmarish quality since her husband is now justified in being unfaithful, throwing her out of the house and/or bringing home another wife.

Women's Role and Place in Society

From childhood a girl is taught that her proper place is the home. The average age of marriage for females is about 13.2 years. Being twenty-five years old I am the object of some curiosity. My colleagues at the university have taken to hiding their real age in order not to block themselves from the marriage market. For the last few years I have been explaining over and over again to numerous relatives, friends and well-wishers that I would prefer to complete my studies and work for a while before marriage. There are tremendous pressures on a woman to conform to the established pattern. It is invariably assumed that she is single not by choice but because no one wishes to marry her. This in turn reflects on her desirability as a wife and mother. People consider her abnormal if she expresses no wish to assume these responsibilities.

Most girls, however, accept the idea that their function is first and foremost to be wives and mothers. When a marriage is arranged, the relatives of the prospective groom come to the house of the girl and subject her to a lengthy interview. Her handiwork is displayed in the form of clothes and embroidered handkerchiefs, tablecoths and pillowcases; the length and quality of her hair are inspected; she is questioned on the best method of cooking an elaborate curry; and among Hindus, her horoscope is also consulted to see if she was born under a lucky star. She herself has virtually no say in the matter. Her knowledge of the facts of life is vague since her mother, out of a mistaken sense of modesty, did not discuss matters freely with her. I have known the case of a young teenager who ran away to her parents within a few weeks of getting married because she was unable to cope with the realities which faced her. I have also seen quite a few young girls who lost their health and good looks within a year of getting married.

Among most of the female students at the universities and colleges there is an attitude of marking time until they can get married. Many of them marry just before their bachelor's or master's degree finals and drop out, simply because their guardians are afraid that if they wait till the exams are over, the man in question (who is probably what is known as a "good catch") will marry some other girl. Even among the well-to-do classes, it is considered essential that a woman get married before she is in the middle twenties.

Working Women

A working woman also encounters many problems. Many an executive expects his secretary to be more than just an efficient helper at the office. Conversely, many people imagine that she is holding her job because of her feminine charms and not her abilities. Nursing is looked down upon and sometimes even the morals of nurses are called into question because the idea of a woman working in close contact with men day and night is something alien to our society, where segregation of the sexes is the norm.

If a woman is single and comes from outside the city she will have accomodation problems, since career women's hostels are few in Dhaka and virtually non-existent in other cities. If she is married she will be, in effect, doing two jobs, since the men of our country consider it demeaning to help in the house. The present government has reserved ten percent of all jobs in the civil service for women, but unless hostels and day care centers for children are built as well, [women] will find it almost impossible to take advantage of this provision.

The Rights of Women Regarding Divorce

Within the institution of marriage, too, women have few rights. The vast majority of people in our country are Muslims and divorce is quick for men but virtually impossible for women.

Sixteen-year old Sitara is a victim of this situation. She lives in a village to the north of Dhaka. Since her father died when she was young it was the duty of the influential men of the village to arrange her marriage, which they did. But her husband, a young man from another village, soon left her and went to Dhaka, where he remarried. Since he had not bothered to divorce Sitara, she cannot get married again and is now living almost as an outcast in her village. . . .

Among the Hindus and Christians, abandonment is more common than divorce, since the Hindus and Roman Catholics do not recognize divorce and, among Protestants, divorce is a long, drawn-out and expensive business.

Prejudice and Discrimination

Among the Christian community, prejudice also takes other forms. In several denominations, the right of women to be ordained is not recognized. Even where it is not, in theory, forbidden, there are almost no women working within the church. One of my aunts, in spite of being appointed pastoral superintendent of her district by her denominational convention, cannot conduct services at the church which she attends. The members of the congregation have objected to a woman in the pulpit. . . .

Religious structures, cultural prejudices, the social and political system have all conspired to keep women in subjugation. Because of this, our men are also not free but forced to play stereotyped roles. They rarely let their womenfolk work outside the home because they fear that it will reflect unfavorably on their abilities as providers. If they do not get rid of this attitude, Bangladesh will continue to be one of the most underdeveloped countries in the world. A country cannot advance with half its population in bondage.

Women's Organizations—Helping or Hindering?

Some organizations in Dhaka and elsewhere are now helping poor women. Many of these organizations are run by women. However women's voluntary associations in our country are regarded with suspicion by some people because these organizations have a reputation of being the playthings of rich women. Except for one or two associations, they mostly seem to lack a sense of direction and the members are content with doing occasional good works, e.g. distributing clothes to the poor. On the other hand, some have well-integrated programs to help poor women earn a living. The organization I am directly involved with, the Y.W.C.A., operates a craft center in Dhaka. It is now also running classes in a village outside the city to teach women to produce these goods in their homes, which are then sold through the Y.W.C.A.

The women's organizations are doing virtually nothing to foster a spirit of solidarity between women. Nothing has been done so far to mobilize opinion in order to change discriminatory laws, to ban polygamy and to protect women from being abused by their husbands. It is only when a woman dies after being assaulted by her spouse that it is reported in the newspapers.

The Changing Situation

It is true, however, that the situation is changing. This change is arising from necessity rather than being born of a realization of the issues involved. More and more women are going out to work because the money earned by the men is no longer sufficient for the family. The biggest catalyst of change was the struggle for independence in 1971. In families where the male members had been killed, the women were forced to seek a job. Women who had been raped and consequently abandoned by their relatives also had to find work to survive.

The process of emancipation is slow but the signs are there. Perhaps the women's pages in the newspapers are a barometer of the change that has taken place. A few years back, they used to be filled with romantic stories, recipes and ways of improving one's looks. Today, the articles are mostly on women's rights in marriage, the working wife's problems and the necessity of higher education for females.

The most important thing, I believe, is a change in attitudes— not only of men, but also of women about themselves and towards each other. Robbed of their dignity, taught to believe from child-hood that they are inferior beings, they try desperately to prove themselves good wives and mothers. One of the characteristics of a group in slavery is that they often try to make life easier for themselves by currying favor with their oppressors. Our women display this in the way they try to win the approval of men, some-times turning against members of their own sex in the process.

However, our rights as women will not be handed to us on a platter. It will take time and much more effort than we, the priv-ileged, are putting in at present. If we think that one fine morning we will wake up and find ourselves liberated, we will find instead that each day the chains around us have tightened just a little more.

SRI LANKA
International Women's Day in Sri Lanka

In recent years it has become a feature of Sri Lanka's multi-faceted, sometimes incomprehensible if not irrational political life that on March 8, celebrated all over the world as International Women's Day, a special brand of violence is used against women. On the one hand there are state-sponsored Women's Day meetings where the rulers pontificate on the virtues of motherhood, the importance of preserving one's femininity while "participating in development" and other similar sentiments. On the other hand policemen and women are given orders to baton-charge, tear-gas, assault and arrest other women from non-governmental organizations who are likewise celebrating Women's Day! Last week, on March 8, 1985, the violence continued.

A Women's Day committee made up of several independent women's organizations had planned to celebrate IWD by holding a public meeting at the New Town Hall on Friday. Since many women belonging to those organizations were expected to travel from various outstations to Colombo on this day, it was decided to gather them together at the De Mel Park in Slave Island and walk in a procession to the New Town Hall. Police permission was sought for the procession as well as for the meeting and monies duly paid for both the park and the hall. On March 7th, in the evening, the committee received a letter from the police commissioner informing them that permission could not be granted for a procession. By then, however, it was far too late to pass on changes in plans to the members.

Accordingly, on March 8, the women proceeded to De Mel Park at 2 p.m. On arriving there they found the police already in possession of the park. After a discussion with the police officers, during which we explained that many of the women who would be coming there would be persons not at all familiar with the city and therefore we had a special responsibility to ensure their safe

Adapted from "Another Violent Women's Day", an article by Sunila Abeysekera that appeared in Lanka Guardian, *March 15, 1985.*

passage to the hall, it was agreed that small groups of women would be allowed to walk along Union Place to the New Town Hall. Accordingly, groups of women were sent off from the park. Despite their original agreement, the members of the committee who were charged with the responsibility of sending off the groups of women from the park, were harassed and even threatened with a cane as if they were mere school children. By 3 p.m., in spite of the fact that several groups of women we were expecting had not yet turned up, the members of the committee were compelled to leave the park.

At about 3:30 p.m. a jeep load of police personnel, men and women, converged on, tear-gassed and attacked a small group of women who had reached the Town Hall area. There was no warning to disperse and scant respect shown for the other persons who happened to be waiting for buses in the bus stands along that stretch of road. One woman suffered a deep wound on her head and had to admitted to the hospital. Four other women were arrested.

Their crime? Using their democratic right of expression to put forward slogans such as: "Bring down the cost of living!" "Mothers of the South join hands with mothers in the North!" "Abolish the law legalizing night work for women!" "Halt the sacrifice of our husbands, fathers and brothers under the cover of the National Question!" "Tear up the new universities bill!" "Abolish the dowry system!" "Enact the proposed legislation granting 3 months maternity leave!"

At 4:30 p.m. the women's organizations of the opposition political parties started a peaceful picket at the Lipton Circus. Their slogans concerned the exploitation of women in the plantations, protested against racism and for national harmony, against rape and violence against women, and called for the protection of women workers in the Middle East. The women involved in this picket campaign included many veterans of the women's movement in our country. They too were set upon with no warning whatsoever, tear-gassed and baton-charged.

It seems incredible that on International Women's Day, which has been celebrated all over the world since 1910, the women of Sri Lanka received only foul language, canings, tear-gas, threats, baton-charges and arrest. As a statement issued by the committee says: "We are surprised and angered at having to be subject to such harassment on a day set aside especially for women in what is supposedly a democratic country. Not only as women but as citizens of this country we strongly condemn the snatching away of our democratic right to the freedom of expression, as well as the violation of our most basic right to walk on the streets of our country without fear of assault and obstruction!"

NEPAL
The Witness of an Illegal Christian

Early in 1985 I had the privilege of being an invited guest at a conference of Nepali-speaking pastors and leaders. There were more than 350 who had registered for the three days of meetings. Excluding the two American guest speakers, there were not more than nine or ten Westerners. People came from Nagaland, Manipur, Mizorham, Assam, Sikkim, Kurseong, North India and various areas of Darjeeling. But by far the greatest number were from Nepal. A few came from Bhutan, another country where the people are not yet allowed to become "legal" Christians.

In order to appreciate the effect this conference had on so many, one need only imagine being one of a handful of Christians in a remote village either in the foothills of the mighty Himalayas or in the flat low-lying areas just north of the Indian border. The gathering of so many who had made a stand for Jesus Christ was a tremendous encouragement and an exciting inspiration. I found myself caught up by the sense of the imminent presence and the power of our great Redeemer as people shared experiences of prison or beatings, or just ostracization for their faith. One was always aware that here was a living Book of Acts!

But the part of the story I most want to share took place the day after the closing of the conference. I was dreading the sixteen-hour all-night ride on an old bus without the slightest resemblance to a Greyhound. I had found only one other person from the conference travelling alone, so we decided to go together.

My young friend [was a] woman of about thirty-five. . . . As we rode through the countryside in the twilight, stopping at each small village along the way, we chatted about many things. I learned that this person's parents had arranged her marriage at the age of

_____

This contemporary story of a Christian Nepali woman comes from the report of a Westerner living in Nepal. Because of the sensitive situation faced by Nepalese Christians the individuals in the story are not further identified.

twelve. A few years later it was discovered that she had early signs of leprosy, and by law it is possible for the husband to leave a wife with that disease and take another (which he did). But in addition, neither mother, father, brothers, nor sisters wanted her any more. She made her own way to the home that treated cases such as hers. During the course of her stay there, she taught herself to read and write and finally decided to place her faith and trust in Jesus Christ. The only effects of this disease are her bent fingertips.

As we talked, she also carried on some small side conversations with one or two others near her on the bus. Then she opened her bag and gave to several of these same people small booklets about the person and purpose of Jesus Christ. She asked each one to kindly pass their booklet on to a friend after they had finished.

A young Brahmin who had also taken one of the pamphlets became furious and heatedly began an argument with her. He fairly shouted with his best high-caste self-assurance that this religion of Jesus Christ and the Bible is not for Nepal and the Nepali people. He made the comment that it is all just for Westerners. Her strong, firm, quiet answer impressed all who were listening. In fact, it seemed at this point that the whole bus-load was her congregation. She simply said that she was a Nepali and a Brahmin as well, and that her faith and belief was in Christ who had healed her, given her new life and filled her with hope for the future. He also began to tell her in no unclear terms that she ought not to be passing out such literature, as it was against the law to do so, and he wanted to know where and how she had gotten those booklets. I must say that I was feeling a bit uncomfortable because of his aggressive attitude. [But] any misgivings I might have had were soon dispelled as she confidently and persistently shared her experience of faith in this new life she had found, and in the One who gave it.

This all went on for a little over an hour when finally we arrived in Kathmandu. As we walked away from the bus we said good-bye to the young man, who was then looking quite embarrassed. I saw four different people come to my friend and warmly and sincerely thank her for all she had shared. As we walked to the taxi, yet another young man came rushing up to ask if he could go with my friend wherever she was going and get more things to read.

It seemed a short trip indeed on that overnight bus . . . a fitting climax to three inspiring days. I knew that if even a few of those attending the conference had gained as much as this dear friend and were able to share, many glorious and wonderful things were in store for the future.

PAKISTAN
Two to One

Since the advent of General Zia's military rule in 1977, the people of Pakistan have found that the army is using Islam as a symbol to perpetuate its despicable hold over the people. The pronouncements of the *mullahs* (religious leaders) on matters relating to minorities—be they religious minorities or women—have caused great anxiety. One of the first arbitrary acts of General Zia's regime was to change the constitution and to introduce a system of "separate electorates" in the country. Under the system, members of minority religions are not allowed to vote for Muslim candidates but for the candidate belonging to their own minority community. This was taken to appease the Muslim fundamentalist party—the *Jamaat-i-Islam*.

The process of Islamization has hit the people, specifically the women, the hardest. To begin with, the women's hockey team was disbanded since women playing hockey in shorts was considered un-Islamic. Female models were banned from appearing in advertizements on television. If they appeared at all, they had to cover their heads, wear high necklines and long sleeves. General Zia's favorite *mullah*, Dr. Israr, made the pronouncement that all working women should be retired and pensioned off.

Other *mullahs* are bringing pressure on the government to repeal the Muslim Family Law ordinance because they consider it un-Islamic. According to the ordinance, a Muslim male cannot marry a second wife without the permission of the courts or the consent of the first wife. According to strict Muslim law, a Muslim male can have four wives at a time. He further has the right to divorce his wives by mere pronouncement of a *tolaq* three times.

To add to the fears of women, the Islamic Ideology Council, set up by the government to bring existing laws into conformity with injunctions of Islam, announced the draft of the Islamic Evidence Act and laws relating to *qisas* (retaliation) and *diyat* (blood money). According to the Islamic Law of Evidence, the evidence of two

From "Pakistan: Islamization and Equality", in Asian Issues, *July 1983, published by the International Affairs division of the Christian Conference of Asia.*

women is equal to that of one man, and in matters relating to *diyat* (compensation), a woman is entitled to only half the compensation of a man.

The changes envisioned in the proposed legislation have outraged many women in Pakistan. Groups like the Women's Action Forum, the Punjab Women Lawyers Association, the Business and Professional Women's Club, the All Pakistan Women's Association and the Women's Social Organization have registered strong protests with the government against the implementation of such laws.

A demonstration of various women's organizations held in Lahore to protest such discriminatory laws was tear-gassed and baton-charged. Thirty-one women demonstrators were held. There were nationwide protests against the action of the police and the martial law authorities.

Although the women are greatly concerned about the intentions of the *mullahs*, who have the support of the regime, some people feel that the raising of the women's issue at this stage is an attempt by the junta to divert public attention away from more pressing and real problems. The junta's minister of information, General Mujubur Rahman, received specialized training in psychological warfare under a scheme sponsored by the Americans. The women of Pakistan, however, feel that the army will not hesitate to curtail their rights in the name of Islam in order to win the support of the *mullahs*.

In an article titled, "Equality before God; Inequality Before the Law!" Hilda Saeeda, a female journalist from *The Star*, a Pakistani English language daily, raises the following points:

"Let us, for a moment, consider briefly some theoretical suppositions which could arise from the proposed Law of Evidence and its repercussions in terms of *qisas* and *diyat*. These suppositions are, however, completely practical and possible. A Muslim man is stabbed in the presence of his mother, his wife and his daughter. A perfectly ordinary occurrence in our crime-ridden society. Is the assaulter to go scot-free because the all-important 'Muslim adult male witness' is missing?

"An economically hard-pressed woman, mother of seven children, is returning home to Chakwara in an overcrowded bus. She has spent the whole day washing utensils and clothes at half a dozen houses. She's on the foot board, precariously balanced; the bus swings into a fast turn, and before the eyes of shocked bus passengers and pedestrians another precious life is lost under the wheels of the monstrous vehicle. However, in the eyes of certain people, not as precious a life as her husband's would have been, had he been the victim. After all, she was not economically as important as he! What possible value could the world attach to her? But had her children been asked, the answer would have been: irreplaceable, beyond value. Will the children grieve less at the death of their mother than at the death of their father? How can less value possibly be attached to one human being and more to another?

"A congregation of Parsees/Hindus/Christians is just coming out of fire temple/mandir/church. They unwittingly observe a gruesome murder or an accident leading to death of the victim. The victim and the murderer/reckless driver, are both Muslim. Is the whole congregation to be blind because it is a population of non-Muslim witnesses?

"Take another hypothetical situation: A *Majlis-e-Shoora* [Parliament] meeting is just over in Islamabad [the capital of Pakistan]. Two members—a man and a woman—are traveling together in the same car. The man is well-off, belongs to a family of landed gentry. The woman, a widow, mother of three school-age children, has by dint of hard work carved out a niche of success for herself. Terrorist attacks are rife. The car is going at a steady pace on Islamabad's smooth, quiet roads and then out of the blue—a flash, a bomb blast. Another vile act of aggression and two valuable lives are lost. Two people who were equally important to their country, to their families—the woman perhaps more so in terms of her children's economic needs. Two people who lost their lives at the very same moment in the very same car, and both on official government duty. Yet the compensation? Something for the man and half of it for the woman."

Let us, for a moment, consider some of the verses pertaining to justice and the ability to bear witness, as stated in the Qu'ran. These are addressed to all believers, not just men and not just women: "O ye who believe! Stand out firmly for justice, as witnesses to God, even as against yourselves, or your parents, or your kin, and whether it be [against] rich or poor. For God can best protect both. Follow not the lust of your hearts lest ye swerve; and if ye distort justice, verily God is well acquainted with all that ye do."

All believers have been addressed here, and justice and equality are considered paramount.

Article 7 of Pakistan's Constitution states: "All are equal before the Law and and are entitled without any discrimination to equal protection of the Law."

Over the years these God-given rights, these Constitution-given rights have been, are being eroded. With what great aim in mind? The improvement and betterment of society? Or the deliberate crippling of well above fifty percent of Pakistan's population?

PEACE, JUSTICE AND MILITARIZATION

Introduction

In southern Asia, as throughout the world, people yearn for a "just peace." Justice means overcoming poverty and achieving the basic human rights of food, education, health and freedom of expression and political will. Achieving peace in southern Asia is crucially intertwined with realizing this justice.

A casual glance at a world map reveals that southern Asia is indeed in the crossroads of major power rivalries. To the north and northeast are the Soviet Union and the People's Republic of China— bitter rivals whose policies greatly affect the people of southern Asia. The U.S.S.R. is a major cause of the conflict in Afghanistan and supplies India with most of its armaments. China, on the other hand, supports the Afghani guerrillas and the Pakistani military government. Pakistan and India have fought three wars in the last four decades and both are thought to be capable of developing nuclear weapons.

To the south and southwest is the Indian Ocean and, beyond it, the Middle East. The Indian Ocean is becoming increasingly militarized, with nuclear weapons-equipped warships and forces— primarily from the United States—poised for action in the Middle East and against the Soviet Union. Within the U.S.-U.S.S.R. struggle the fabric of two countries, Afghanistan and Pakistan, is being torn apart. Thousands have perished since the Soviets intervened in Afghanistan in 1979. Now, Pakistan, with outside assistance, supports the largest refugee camps in the world. Yet in Pakistan a military government largely supported by U.S. military and economic assistance severely violates human rights.

Outside military influences greatly exacerbate many of the region's "built-in" tensions, such as ethnic violence, endemic poverty and struggles for greater political autonomy. Precious human and material resources are diverted from the work of development to police and military sectors.

The plan to make the Indian Ocean a "zone of peace" represents a regionally-determined, United Nations-backed blueprint for demilitarization of the region. The superpowers must back away from southern Asia to let justice take its course and to let the countries of the region determine their own destinies.

Churches in southern Asia are a distinct minority; they literally face the cross in working for a just peace. In each country Christians are up against different realities in dealing with the tidal waves of militarization and injustice. Our knowledge of these realities is crucial to our understanding of the churches in this region.

* * * *

Written by Chandran Devansen, the following is a meditation on an ancient Sanskrit prayer for liberation. The Sanskrit words are from the Upanishads, *written in India about 300 B.C. The translation is in italics. Reprinted from* CCA News, *February 1985.*

Asato ma sad gamaya

Out of untruth lead us into truth.

Lord, hear the cry of the civilized.

Lead us from the untruth in the mouth of the gun, the barking, sputtering gun, the gun that silences the still, small, voice of justice; the gun which in the hands of the oppressed turns into the tyrant's bayonet in the belly of the people.

Lead us from the untruth in the burr and whirr, the clack and clatter of the Machine when it is made to grind the people; from the smoke and soot, the cotton and dust which coughs the blood from the lungs of the workers.

Lead us from the untruth of false ideals which drag history in the mud, and set our feet upon the road of truth.

Tamaso ma jyotir gamaya

Out of darkness lead us into light.

Lord, lead us out of the darkness of the *kisan's* house of mud, the sweeper's home of kerosene tins, and the *chawls* and *bustees* of the factory worker, into the light of airy room and spacious parks, and the sound of children playing in open spaces.

Lead us out of the darkness of the darkened mind which grades man by *namam* and *varnam* into high caste and low caste, the darkness of the hand outstretched to Thee which will not touch the skill of the *chuklis* and *pariahs*, the darkness of men who see refuge in Thy shadow but refuse Thee in the shadow of Thy poor and lowly.

Lead us out of the darkness that plunges the girl into the darkness of an old man's desire, the darkness of the girl—pawn in the dowry shop; the darkness of the child robbed of her youth, of her years blossoming into womanhood.

Lead us from the darkness of bondage into the light of freedom in the world of nations.

Lead us from the darkness of our today into the light of Thy tomorrow.

Mrityor ma mritam gamaya

Out of death lead us into eternity

Lord, out of the death of evil thinking and evil doing, lead us into the eternity of the good life.

Out of the death of our whole bodies lead us into the eternity of the life of the race which springs from our flesh.

Lead us out of the death of the seen into the eternity of the Unseen. When death approaches may we cry, Santi! Santi! Santi! Peace, deep peace, and so pass into the eternity of the deathless mind which is in the form of all things.

Glossary:
   kisan: peasant
   chawls and *bustees:* slums
   namam: caste mark
   varnam: caste (literally, color)
   chuklis: leather workers
   pariahs: untouchables

PAKISTAN
Militarization in Pakistan
by Dr. Feroz Ahmed

In looking at militarization in Pakistan there are two important questions:

1. What are the internal reasons and forces that have facilitated the process of militarization?
2. What has been the role of the U.S. in the militarization of Pakistan?

We cannot view these two inquiries separately.

Pakistan is a country of 85 million people. Its armed or regular forces are close to one-half million, according to the latest [1983] reports . . . Plus there are other kinds of divisions [apart from] the regular forces. The official current military expenditure is about $1 billion a year. Officially, it comprises about 40 percent of the budget. Based on my own research, I know that this percentage is highly understated.

Foreign military assistance comes to Pakistan from the U.S. in the amount of about $3.2 billion extended over a period of about six years. And the first squadron of F-16's, the most sophisticated of U.S. fighter bombers, has already been delivered. Pakistan has been ruled by a military regime for the last six years. This has been the third nationwide martial law instituted in Pakistan. A "selective" martial law preceded this one. After the Bangladeshi conflict [1971], an elected civilian government ruled for about five and one half years. Then the army stepped in under the pretext of maintaining order and holding free and fair elections within ninety days.

Dr. Ahmed is a former professor at Sind University in Pakistan and editor of the opposition publication, Pakistan Forum. *He is now in exile in the United States. This is an edited transcript of a presentation he made in April, 1983 to the Task Force on Militarization in Asia and the Pacific of the National Council of the Churches of Christ in the USA.*

The ninety days have been stretched to today and there is yet no sign of the military stepping down.

There is a direct relationship between the militarization of Pakistan and politics. This relationship starts from the very early 1950's. Pakistan was created in 1947. Pakistan was a new state in a post-colonial period at a time when states were coming into being. Unlike India, where you have a very strong nationalistic upper class, (and a large middle class that shares upper-class and nationalist sentiments) Pakistan did not have a strong upper class and its landlord class proved itself incapable of holding state power. What existed was an enormous civilian bureaucracy and a military with a lot of potential growth. The bureaucracy and the military were the real depositories of power. The landlords, therefore, became quite dependent upon the bureaucrats. A capitalist upper class began to emerge, but it also became dependent upon the civilian bureaucracy. The bureaucracy, therefore, had enormous power and the military the potential for that. As the power struggle was going on for constitutional concerns, the U.S., under the cold war strategy of Secretary of State John Foster Dulles, was looking for allies around the world. Pakistan was strategically seen as a very important country as it borders China, almost borders the Soviet Union, is at the mouth of the Persian Gulf, and has a border with Iran.

Pakistan was brought into two multi-lateral pacts—SEATO and CENTO; a bilateral treaty with the U.S. in 1954 and, later on, another U.S. bilateral agreement in 1959. Pakistan allowed the use of its airfields for U2 spy missions on the Soviet Union. U.S. strategic concerns were harmonious with the desire of the Pakistani military to capture power. This marriage of interests also involved the upper classes, who were dependent on the Pakistani military.

The whole military ruling elite wanted allies from outside to safeguard their power as they certainly were not satisfying the aspirations of the Pakistani people. It is important to note that the U.S. did not become an inadvertent tool in militarization of Pakistani politics and society simply because of its strategic interest. That is only one aspect of it. The U.S. consciously, deliberately and premeditatively tried to build up the Pakistani army into a political institution. A quote from a joint report of Department of State and Department of Defense Mutual Security Program 1958-62 states: "From a political viewpoint, U.S. military aid has strengthened Pakistan's armed services as the greatest stabilizing force in the country and has encouraged Pakistan to participate in collective defensive agreements."

From 5,000 to 6,000 Pakistani officers have been trained by the U.S. military, some of them in counterinsurgency and psychological warfare. This psychological warfare is being turned against the people of Pakistan right now. The post of Secretary of Information, which is a key position, is held by General Rahman. He was trained by the CIA in psychological warfare and he is using all the tactics of psychological warfare to disorient the people of Pakistan and keep them in slavery.

[A spokesperson] for the U.S. State Department states four advantages for improving security relations with Pakistan:

1. The denial of Pakistani territory to the U.S.S.R.;
2. To aid Afghan rebels militarily to raise the cost of Soviet intervention. (Few people realize that Pakistan began to intervene in Afghan affairs in May of 1978, nineteen months prior to the full-scale Soviet intervention);
3. The use of Pakistani facilities in connection with the planned Rapid Deployment forces. (This is now called the Central Command. With this, there has been talk of using the Port of Karachi and a port on the Pakistani coast where Pakistani military personnel are currently being supervised by Americans); and
4. The demonstration of American security reliability, especially with respect to the People's Republic of China.

Pakistan has been very important for U.S. strategies beginning with Dulles's Cold War policies, through the "Nixon Doctrine" (that is, developing surrogate or client states to implement U.S. military policy) and into the Reagan Administration's global military buildup, especially in the Indian Ocean. This cost has been heavy to the people of Pakistan. It has prolonged their agony and has recently given a new lease on life to the military dictatorship. It has also endangered Pakistan's security. The U.S. is 12,000 miles away and the Soviet Union is a next-door neighbor. Pakistani coexistence has to be worked out with the Soviet Union. But the fact is that Pakistan has provoked the Soviet Union right from the beginning with America's support. The Soviet Union may, indeed, have its own designs. But the facts show that the Soviet Union has not yet done anything really to endanger the peace of Pakistan. It may have reason to invade Pakistan considering Pakistan's new armaments and Pakistani destabilization efforts in Afghanistan. Given Pakistan's subservience to American interests, the danger of the Soviet Union acting against Pakistan always exists.

INDIA
A Social Action Agenda for Indian Churches

"... the institutional church has some constraints in moving easily into all the areas of struggle for justice, [but] it is imperative for the churches to provide support to the social action groups which are directly involved in the struggle for the oppressed. ..."

So reads, in part, a statement issued by a recent consultation on the church and social action groups in India. It is a significant statement because although it mentions the deeply-rooted "constraints" which have kept Indian churches out of many public issues, it recognizes the ongoing work of Christian social action groups. Another statement was issued in 1984 by the Commission on Justice and Peace of the Joint Council of Three Indian Churches. These churches, which together claim some three and a half million members, are the Church of North India, the Church of South India and the Mar Thoma Syrian Church. While giving the somewhat false impression that there had been few significant Christian social action initiatives up until then, the commission's statement is an important indication of the interest the church is now taking in the public issues of the day. The recommendations it makes cover a wide range of issues, such as: the 1869 Indian Divorce Act, interfaith marriages, dowry, socio-economic issues and caste issues. Some of the actions taken are described in summary below:

- The *Indian Divorce Act of 1869* was said to be "archaic, oppressive and discriminatory as between men and women, and as between some Christians and others." The Commission concluded that the act "has to be studied fully and revised . . . with the Indian Christian Marriage Act."
- On *interfaith marriages* the Commission noted that these ". . . will increase, and asks the churches and the Christian community to accept them with love, understanding and pastoral responsibility." It also expressed "concern that social drinking is

From CCA News, *September 15, 1984.*

gaining increasing respectability and that the menace of drug addiction was growing. . . "

- *Dowry,* the Commission stated, ". . . contradicts the plan of the Creator who instituted marriage as a convenantal relationship between man and woman. . . "

- On *socio-economic political issues:* "We believe that the church's concern for socio-economic political issues of the society of which it is a part arises from its very nature of being called to be the 'salt of the earth', 'light of the world', and the 'leaven' in the society. This concern should lead the church to get involved in actions for restructuring society towards the coming into being of a new humanity in Christ."

- On *caste issues:* ". . . the member churches . . . [should] be urgently concerned about the plight and problems of the outcaste people [scheduled castes and tribes], both within and outside the Christian fold, as a priority for the mission of the church in India. . . . First priority . . . must be given to those inside the Church. . . . [the member churches should] take immediate initiatives, such as the following, in support of the struggles and liberation movements of the outcaste people:

  a) synod-level commissions for study and action on caste issues;

  b) initiate action programs for creating self-awareness and self-understanding among our rural illiterate and poverty-stricken Christian outcaste people, so that it will lead to changing the existing power structures at the local pastorate or parish level;

  c) create and operate a support fund for outcasts at the synod level, specifically providing scholarships and financial assistance for developing and promoting leadership among the outcaste people.

BANGLADESH
A Young Person's View
of Militarization

Karuna sat on the floor surveying the array of articles, papers, notes and pictures surrounding her. Would she ever be able to write a script to go with the slides which had just arrived? Would she find adequate words to share all she had learned and experienced at the CCA* conference she had just attended in Japan? She wanted to be able to write about the deep feelings she had experienced as one of a small group who had traveled to Hiroshima and participated in the August 6th memorial service. Each time Karuna had tried to tell her family of that experience she got choked up. Even her own experience in the Bangladesh civil war had not prepared her for Hiroshima. She had understood the banners carried in the memorial procession which read: "Never Again—No More Hiroshimas!" but found it difficult to share what had so moved her.

Perhaps she should start with this experience at Hiroshima.

"Draft Script on Militarization in South Asia" (she wrote)

[PICTURE]	[SCRIPT]
Peace Memorial Service	Hiroshima was where I started with a small group who participated in the Asia Youth Resource Conference. The experience led the participants to make a statement which ended with these words:
Procession with banners	"Hiroshima, we remember your agony but not with sentiment for the past which blinds us to the realities of the present. We remember you instead with our anger at the continuing oppression by the U.S. and Japan. We remember you instead with our demands for peace based, not just on
Youth reading statement	

*Christian Conference of Asia

Written by Barbara H. Chase, this fictitious account is based on material from actual youth conferences recently held in Asia and North America.

nuclear disarmament, but on global justice and the right of all people to self-determination."[1]

Japanese delegates speaking at the conference

I was very moved by the Japanese delegates who were willing to expose their own country's exploitation and who were actively working to make a difference. In fact, it was not so much the written papers which made an impression on me, as the people who were so committed to ridding their countries of militaristic attitudes and policies.

Close-up of conference participants, showing the different nationalities and representatives of clergy and lay leaders, both women and men

Just why were we gathered? What was the purpose of such a conference? The leader of the conference put it this way: ". . . to link the Asian ecumenical youth movement more closely with the people's movements and action groups which are dealing with the urgent issues of our day. It also aims to bring the agenda of militarization more firmly into the churches to ensure an adequate Christian response."[2]

Military police in Pakistan, in India, in Sri Lanka

" Militarization — Afraid of the People"—that was the theme of one speech. In summary, the speaker said that "Asian societies are becoming militarized to an unprecedented degree. This is a response of fear in the face of growing people's resistance. Globally integrated systems of exploitation now require globally integrated systems of suppression.[3]

Police on school grounds, on busy streets

Tanks parked on street corners

" Militarization means more than the increase in weapons and military technology, which is normally justified by invoking a foreign threat while the intended use of new instruments of war is to silence the national citizenry. Such increases are taking place, and very rapidly. However, militarization extends to every aspect of social life and to a nation's institutions.[4]

Military
police in India
with tear-gas

Government
leaders in
session

Family in
front of a
jail seeking
information on
a relative
in prison

Nuclear plant
in India

Nuclear station
in Pakistan

Police arrest
tea estate
workers

Workers in the
tea estates

"Militarization is a declaration of war by a state on its own people. The government leadership need not always be military personnel for this declaration to be made. In some Asian countries, governments maintain a civilian facade and often keep up the appearance of a parliamentary democracy where people vote.

"Abuses of human rights are inevitable in this war as people are arbitrarily detained, tortured and killed. Politics is not a contest for the confidence of the people. It becomes a process of eliminating all opposition."[5]

"Nuclearization"—It was difficult for me to even say this word, but by the end of the conference I had certainly learned!

"Nuclearization is the most recent process whereby the militarization of Asia is pursued." In East Asia and the Pacific, the military bases and nuclear power plants were very controversial. Governments said they brought jobs to the needy, while activist groups said the needy were exploited by being submitted to such high-risk jobs! Conference delegates from Pakistan seemed to understand this fear but theirs was of the unknown, since information on nuclear research and the possibility of a nuclear bomb is not available.[6]

Why increased military power? In a report from Sri Lanka, the point was made that external military threats are given as reasons by national governments for increasing military power, but the reality is that this is an excuse to strengthen the arm of the state against the rising discontent of the people. In Sri Lanka this is seen as linked with the ethnic conflict between the Tamils and Sinhalese. When the Prevention of Terrorism Act was reintroduced in 1982, it was as if the terrorism of the armed forces against the Tamils were legalized.[7]

Youth are
rounded up

One of the youth from Sri Lanka reported that "terrorism" was so loosely defined that the armed forces could detain a suspect for eighteen months without a trial in an unknown place and without access to lawyers, friends or family. It was also reported that the present government (1983) increased military spending from 500 million rupees in 1977 to 1.2 billion rupees in 1980! While the Tamils have felt the brunt of this, it is recognized that the Sinhalese peasants are also duped by the government and suffer similar oppression.[8]

Karuna paused in her preparation of the script and wondered if the web created by militarism would ever be untangled. She felt strength in knowing that other youth were concerned and actively trying to bring about change in their nations. But it was a lonely journey and Karuna wondered if she would be able to rally the youth of her city for any kind of action.

Western office
buildings in
Sri Lanka,
Pakistan, India,
Bangladesh

People sleeping
and living on
the streets in
Bombay

Military parade
in Pakistan

Market scene
with many
Western gadgets,
appliances

Transnational corporations— The report on transnational corporations (TNC's) and militarization listed a number of problems which came along with TNC's: pollution; exploitation of workers, especially youth and women; impoverishment of the people and their land; military production by TNC's; and militarization.

A speaker pointed out that ". . . third world countries are militarizing to protect TNC economic interests . . . [this] is also creating an exodus of landless farmers to urban areas. . . . massive consumerism [is introduced for] unnecessary consumer products."[9]

It was horrible to grasp from all the statistics presented how large a percentage of a country's resources of people and money are expended on the military.

Where do we go from here? What can we do with all the information and new insights gained from such a gathering? In one of the final sessions, we reviewed our task theologically. We spent time in prayer, meditation and worship as a group of young people prepared to put the practical application of love in the political processes of our countries.

Conference at prayer, at worship, singing

SRI LANKA
Women for Peace

"Women for Peace," a non-partisan organization, was created in December 1984 to bring together women to demand a peaceful, negotiated, political— as opposed to a military—settlement to the civil war in Sri Lanka. Having collected over ten thousand signatures, they have decided to initiate a "consciousness raising" program.

An appeal from women cries out that Sri Lanka is being destroyed and women must speak out. "To abdicate participation in the most critical political issue of the day is to affirm the reactionary idea that the public sphere is man's domain and the domestic sphere the woman's. Violence, once concentrated on the north, is inexorably spreading to encompass the whole island like an ever-widening stain of blood. As the economy grinds to a halt in the north, women live in fear of assault and the disappearance and death of their men. In the south, all resources are directed towards the war machine, and the biggest employer is the army. Sri Lanka is condemning its youth to death and exile."

A Tamil Mother in the North

I am a widow of fifty-two, with five sons and one daughter. In May of this year unbelievable tragedy struck our family. When I think over the events of those two terrible weeks I am gripped by a sense of unreality.

We had just sat down to lunch that day when five army officers knocked on the front door and said they wanted to talk to my youngest son. My son was not at home, so they told me to send him to the army camp at the Jaffna Stadium as soon as he came home. I was worried but tried not to show it when I told my son this. He reassured me and said he would go straightaway since he had nothing to hide. We decided he should go to the nearest police station since they were the civil authorities concerned. Later, I heard that the police had sent him over to the army camp at the stadium.

My son did not return home that night and I was sleepless with

From personal testimonies that appeared in the Spring/Summer 1985 issue of Lanka Review.

worry. In the morning, I went to the camp to inquire about my son, but they refused to let me see him. That evening I heard a rumor that he had been taken to a hospital. When I rushed to the hospital, I heard he had been moved against medical advice. No one could tell me where he was. At home everybody tried to comfort me. But how could I stop worrying until I saw my son again?

It was exactly two weeks later that a policeman arrived at our house. At last, I thought hopefully, he would be able to tell me about my son. He did. He told me abruptly that my son was dead and that I must go to Colombo for the post-mortem. I could only stare at him in disbelief. He did not even tell me how my son had died and I could not think to ask him any questions.

The next day I went to Colombo with this policeman. At the hospital they took me straight to the mortuary. My son's body was wrapped in a cloth and only his face was visible. He had already been dead for ten days and his face was swollen and discoloured. They asked me to identify him. They would not uncover the rest of his body and a hundred anguished questions flooded my mind. How did my son die? Why didn't they show me his body? Were they afraid to show my how my son had died? I was told that the post-mortem was already over and that an inquest would be held. The inquest began almost immediately. However, soon after I had begun giving evidence the authorities decided to postpone it for a week. They advised me to go back to Jaffna.

The inquest was never resumed. I still do not know why he was killed, nor who killed him. Perhaps those who killed him were no older than he was.

Why must our sons kill each other like this? It is said that your sons kill our sons because our sons kill yours. Yet this is not a problem that can be resolved by your sons and our sons killing each other. This is a problem that was created by politicians and it is they who must resolve it. Let us all stand together as mothers and ask for an end to this killing. Today everyone is talking of the war in our country. They collect money, they donate blood, they honor members of the forces, they perform *bodhi-poojas*, all to ensure victory in this war. Yet I am a mother of a son who was sacrificed in this war. Please listen to my story.

A Sinhalese Mother in the South

I have four sons. My husband served as a police constable for twenty-six years and retired last year. He never stooped to underhanded ways to secure promotions, nor did he take bribes and get innocent persons into trouble. He had a difficult life on his meager salary. Since he was frequently transferred, our children's education suffered.

My eldest son was only able to pass four subjects in the "O" Level exam. He left school because of financial difficulties and tried to find a job. After months of chasing after important people, sending in job applications and going into interviews he was still unable to find anything. Finally, though his father was very much against the idea, he applied to the police. His first appointment was in Colombo, where he served for five years. He tried desperately to get a transfer closer to home, especially since he was planning to get married soon. But when the transfer came it was for compulsory service in the north.

On the day before he left home we all went to the village temple. There we made a vow to the *Kataragama Deviyo* to protect him. My son saw the tears on my cheeks and said jokingly, "Amma, You're crying as if it was my funeral." He put his arm around my shoulders and reassured me that he would come home safely.

From that day we waited eagerly for letters from him. With what apprehension we read the newspapers and listened to the radio announcing happenings in the north. How we longed for the day when my son would be safely home.

One day, returning home from the market, I saw a police jeep parked outside our house. I hurried home excitedly, thinking our son must have come home unexpectedly. It had been so long since I had last seen his face. When I went inside there were police officers I did not recognize. Nobody said anything. Everyone stared into space. At once I knew something was wrong. I looked at my husband's face and realized something terrible had happened to my son. He took me aside, muttered something about an accident and led me into the bedroom. My legs were shaking. I sat on the bed. I heard voices saying that the jeep was blown sky high.

Three days later they brought his remains home. The lid of the coffin was nailed shut. On the lid was a thick square of glass through which the resemblance of a human face could be made out. Was that my son? How unfortunate I am that I could not see my son's face for the last time. At the funeral I heard someone say, "These people are lucky. Sometimes there is nobody to send, only little pieces."

Why do our children have to die like this? I know my son was sent to the north to catch those who are called "terrorists" or to kill them. And so our children end up killing each other and it is we, mothers, who have to live with this unbearable sorrow.

At the funeral a monk made a speech saying, "How fortunate you are to be the mother who gave this son to defend our country, our nation and our religion." But should I be proud to have sent my son to die in this meaningless war? Whose war is this?

INDIAN OCEAN
A Vision For Demilitarization
by the Rev. Tony Watkins

The issue of an Indian Ocean peace zone was first raised in 1964 by Sri Lanka (then Ceylon) at the Cairo Second Conference of Non-aligned Nations. Seven years later, the peace zone concept was sanctioned overwhelmingly by the U.N. General Assembly, which formed an Ad Hoc Indian Ocean Committee to guide discussions toward implementation. Between 1972 and 1979, steady progress was made by regional states in clarifying diverse definitions of: the geographical area to be covered by the zone of peace; the nature of foreign "non-regional" great power military presence; weapons denuclearization; regional security assurrances; peaceful settlements of disputes; and use of the ocean by foreign vessels and aircraft. By March of 1977, the Carter Administration entered into bilateral consultations with the Soviets, proposing that as a matter of first import, "the Indian Ocean be completely demilitarized." These talks proceeded smoothly until the summer of 1978 when they were abruptly broken off by the U.S. side, which acted on recommendations from the Joint Chiefs of Staff, who by then had come to feel that the Zone of Peace (ZOP) concept was a potentially dangerous notion that would threaten future U.S. military posture in the northwest Indian Ocean shoreline. It is important to note that this position preceeded the fall of the Shah and Soviet troop intervention in Afghanistan.

The U.N. Declaration of the Indian Ocean as a ZOP on its face is not complex and simply calls for: 1) the great powers (the U.S., the U.S.S.R., France and Britain) to halt further escalation and expansion of their military presence in the Indian Ocean; 2) elimination of all bases, military installations, logistical supply facilities, nuclear weapons and other weapons of mass destruction from the region which are conceived in the context of great power rivalry; 3) the establishment of collective regional security and cooperation without military blocks; 4) the removal of all warships and military

---

The Rev. Tony Watkins represents the organization Clergy and Laity Concerned. This article is adapted and edited from his manuscript, "Northwest Indian Ocean: New Theater for Global War or Zone of Peace?"

72

aircraft which may be employed to threaten or actually use force against the sovereignty, territorial integrity or independence of any shoreline or inland state.

The Declaration's simplicity, from the point of view of the U.S. and the U.S.S.R., has been problematic for different reasons. Since the cancellation of the U.S.-Soviet talks on the Indian Ocean, the U.S. has maintained that its greatest concern with the ZOP concept is its purported restrictions on the international right of freedom for foreign ships to navigate and for aircraft to fly over the ocean, including warships and aircraft. The Reagan Administration sees fit not to sign the recently-passed U.N. Convention on the Law of the Sea for similar reasons. Yet regional states have repeatedly reaffirmed the right of all states "to use the Indian Ocean for navigation and other *peaceful purposes* freely and without hindrance."

The U.S.S.R. has problems with the ZOP concept because the term "great power rivalry" is used. Some of the Third World states in the region seek to hold the great powers equally responsible for the continued arms escalation. The Soviets claim that they are not military rivals with the U.S. or any other nation "in this or any other part of the world."

The ZOP concept is different from the question of regional nuclear-free zones. While the ZOP includes weapons denuclearization it also addresses broader issues, such as the elimination from the area of other weapons of mass destruction (chemical and biological weapons), and it emphasizes a nuclear arms rivalry between extra-regional great powers who are currently engaged in a dangerous arms buildup in the Indian Ocean. This particular aspect of the ZOP concept is fraught with problems, such as the standing disagreement between Pakistan and India. Pakistan, since 1974, has pushed hard for a nuclear-free zone in South Asia while India is reluctant to agree because it feels surrounded by nuclear weapons powers who are not part of the geographical region.

Both the U.S. and the U.S.S.R. support Indian Ocean weapons denuclearization but in somewhat divergent ways. The U.S. opposes nuclear proliferation by states in the region (Pakistan, Israel, India and South Africa) and supports regional nuclear-free zones, but stops short of serious discussion about the removal of its own nuclear forces or of giving shoreline states any assurances that it will refrain from being the first to use nuclear weapons against them. The Soviets also support a regional nuclear-free zone and oppose proliferation by states in the region. They differ from the U.S. in being ready to discuss removal of their nuclear weapons and in their willingness to pledge to all states in the region a non-first use of nuclear weapons.

BANGLADESH
Education and Development in Bangladesh

A Woman

In rural Bangladesh it is not proper for a wife to bring the name of her husband to her lips. Shamela Begum was predictably silent when we asked her, but another woman beside her furnished the name: "Rahmat Ali". However Shamela did not hesitate to talk about other things relating to her family.

Shamela and Rahmat have three daughters and two sons. Shamela narrated, rather than giving the age of her eldest, a daughter now married and living with her husband. She explained: "You see that date palm there? It was first cut for juice the same year my eldest daughter was born." On counting we found nineteen cuttings on the date palm; therefore the daughter is now nineteen years old. The youngest, a son, is eight. "He was born in the year after the liberation war [1971]," Shamela explained.

Rahmat is a laborer. He works for others as a farmer, mends houses, carries goods, etc. He gets work almost every day and his earnings range from 10 to 14 *taka* for a day's work.*

Shamela, on the other hand, apart from housekeeping, has her hands full with different kinds of work. She does a little rice growing and vegetable gardening on a small plot of land beside the house. But what is interesting is that she has become a member of a women's association called "Dheki-kula Samity", organized by the Shivalaya Rural Development Program (SRDP) of the Christian Commission for Development in Bangladesh (CCDB).

Paddy husking is the association's main project. SRDP funded the association's purchase of a couple of husking paddles; members

*US $1 = 26 *taka*.

The stories in this chapter are adapted from reports written by Shamim Akhtar, information officer of the Christian Commission for Development in Bangladesh (CCDB). They come out of visits to the Shivalaya Rural Development Program (SRDP) which CCDB has been operating in the Shavalaya and Harirampur thanas, about fifty miles west of Dhaka.

of the association can take loans from SRDP to purchase paddy for husking and then sell the rice to make a profit. Shamela said that she can husk about a *maund* (approximately 85 pounds) of paddy in one day. She earns about 7 *taka* per *maund*.

The association also has a savings scheme. The members deposit 5 to 10 *taka* as they can. In the last five months they saved 505 *taka*, which was used to purchase three *maunds* of *kaloi* (a kind of pulse). Presently, the association members are engaged in learning sericulture, for which the SRDP has provided a female trainer. "I am learning too," said Shamela.

The children also make small contributions toward the family. They attend school in an SRDP children's center; they also do odd jobs in exchange for a meal or a few *poisas*. The children have to look after the rearing of a calf, a she-goat and four hens. These have been taken by the family on a sharing basis from their owners. For the calf, the family will pay 930 *taka* when it grows up and is sold; they expect to sell it for 1500 *taka* and the excess amount will be their profit. The goat will be returned after offspring are born; they will get equal share of the kids. If only one kid is born it will be sold and the amount equally divided. As for the hens, the eggs are being preserved for hatching. The hens also have to be returned to the owner after chicks are born, which will be shared equally.

About food, Shamela said: "It is not easy for us to have square meals every day, but we manage somehow." The family's most common meals are *khichuri*, a mixture of rice and lentils cooked together, and *panta-bhat*, cooked rice soaked in water overnight, which is then eaten with chillies and salt. At times they eat *shaag*, a leafy vegetable collected from the surrounding area. *Ata rooti*, handmade wheat flour bread, has to be eaten as well, for it is not possible to buy rice every day. Sometimes the family eats small fish if they can afford them or if the children fish some out of the nearby ditches and ponds.

The discussion finally moved towards family planning. When asked whether she wants more children, Shamela said that she does not and neither does her husband. Although she said that she is taking herbal medicine to control birth, she added, with a sigh, a village proverb: "*Shob haraiyya bilaiyya boishtomi!*" meaning something like, "pauper after losing and giving everything."

Whatever her philosophy may be arising out of the family planning question, Shamela seemed to have a lot of hope.

* * *

A Young Man

Al Hakim Miza, 27 years old, is a teacher at the Shivalaya Central Primary School. This young man has also played a major role in the formation of a number of landless laborers' associations under the Shivalaya Rural Development Program. He is not a staff member of the SRDP. He is an unpaid volunteer.

It was in his own area, Tepra, that the first landless association was formed. Hakim, with a few of his friends, gave leadership and organized as many as 127 members. The activites of the association are sugarcane and rice cultivation, rickshaw-pulling, fish farming and fruit tree planting. Also included is adult education and discussion on family planning.

A loan of 8941 *taka* was given by SRDP, repayable in three years. Two years have gone by, but as Hakim said, "I am confident that we will repay early next year and make a profit for the association."

The rickshaw-pulling project is for members of the association who are not involved in the sugarcane project and have no regular job. "Part of the income from the rickshaws is set aside and saved by the association for purchasing additional rickshaws, which will support other members," said Hakim. He relates a story of what happened a year and a half ago between the landless laborers of the area and a landowner:

"It so happened that a certain landowner wanted to have a canal dug. The laborers were contacted and offered the usual 7 *taka* each for a day's work. They said this was not a fair wage and demanded 15 *taka*. When the owner refused, they went on strike. Then the owner contacted laborers from another area and hired them. But when the local laborers heard about this they approached the neighboring laborers and explained that they were fighting for their rights. If others now worked in this area, all their efforts would go in vain. The second party is said to have understood the situation and withdrew without working for the landowner. The landowner could find no other option but to hire the local laborers. There was further negotiation on the question of the daily wage; both parties came to an understanding and agreed on 12 *taka*."

Hakim lives with his mother, a sister and a brother in his own home surrounded by a small plot of land. He has no major cultivable land. Each morning Hakim raises early, washes himself and prays to Allah. Between 5:30 a.m. and 9 a.m. he tends the plants that grow in his little plot. Then he reads a little. Soon after, he takes a light breakfast, usually handmade bread and vegetables. He goes on doing chores and just before leaving for school, which begins at 10 a.m., he eats rice, curry and *dal* (lentils). On his way to the school he follows a routine, meeting members of the association and visiting the sugarcane field. He works in school from 10 a.m. to 4 p.m. with a half-hour break for a lunch of tea and biscuits. He has to work six days a week and gets a salary of 435 *taka* per month.

"The amount barely makes ends meet," Hakim said, but added, "It keeps me, my mother, brother and sister going."

He takes about an hour returning home from school, following the same routine as in the morning. At home he washes, has a meal of rice, curry and *dal* once again. Around 6 p.m. he goes to the association center, a bamboo house donated by the SRDP, where he is sure to find a couple of members. They talk informally. At 7, other members pour in, quite a few of them bringing lighted lanterns, which are used to light the house and to help people see their way in the dark. They discuss the day's activities, the problems and achievements they may have had. Three nights are given over to adult education classes, the literate members teaching the illiterate ones. They stay up to 10 p.m. Some nights, the members visit other associations to exchange ideas and experiences.

We learned that Hakim does his share in the sugarcane field on Friday, the day school is closed. When asked why he became a volunteer, giving so much time to the association when he could do something else to earn more, Hakim smiled.

"I enjoy working with the landless. I am landless too, you know. It is true that I and a few other members could become private tutors to earn more and live a little better, but the pleasure of working together with my neighbors and friends is far greater than doing something all alone."

The youthful Hakim, SRDP volunteer, school teacher, member of the association, farmer, wants to have a better life jointly with his neighbors.

* * *

A Health Care Worker

Aseea Khatton is a widow of 45. She has a son who is learning to be a salesman in a shop and four daughters, three of whom are married; Aseea is on the lookout for a good husband for the last. The house the family lives in is her own. She cultivates six decimal of land with her son. Since the last storm the family has been living in the kitchen, which is separate from the main hut, since the roof and walls of the house were blown away. As we spoke, Aseea's daughter appeared with two large glasses of fresh coconut water—she had not forgotten the local custom of entertaining her guests.

One thing I observed about Aseea was that all the time we spoke she clutched a white cloth bag which looked like a pillow slip. She never let go of it. It was only when we asked her about it that she revealed its contents: a razor blade, a bottle with some liquid in it, a plastic container of cotton, a notebook and a cake of soap—all items she needs when delivering a baby.

Aseea Khatoon has been a *dai* for fifteen years. *Dais* are traditional midwives, or birth attendants. For the last four years Aseea has served under the Companyganj Health Project (CHP), which was begun by the Christian Commission for Development in Bangladesh (CCDB), funded by such organizations as the World Council of Churches, Christian Aid in Great Britain, the Ford Foundation and UNICEF. The reason for the program is based on the experience that in rural Bangladesh, attendance of women for antenatal services is practically nil. The CHP trains *dais* in order to promote safe deliveries at home, to increase their knowledge of the complications of pregnancy and labor and when to refer patients to the hospital. *Dais* are also taught to impart knowledge to mothers about nutrition and to advise them about prevention of further childbirth.

Since working with CHP, Aseea's style of operation has greatly changed. Previously, although *dais* used clean old clothes for deliveries, they did not have the needed knowledge about sanitation and cleanliness. They visited pregnant woman only when they were in labor, to deliver the baby. They seldom did any antenatal or postnatal checkups. Some *dais* said that pregnant women should not eat much, otherwise the baby would become big and cause difficulty in delivery. As soon as the baby was delivered it was left on a mat on the floor until the placenta was delivered, then the cord was cut with a shaving blade, knife, pair of scissors or even a piece of bamboo. Convulsions or spasms or lockjaw in newborns were believed to be caused by evil spirits.

CHP training attempted to correct only those practices and beliefs which were felt to be clearly harmful. The new system was very encouraging. It was not hard, first of all, for the *dais* to make contact with pregnant women to give them antenatal advice. If the *dais* encountered complications they referred the case to the nearest clinic or hospital. They were also to maintain a record of their activities, which was written by some literate neighbor. And every week all of the *dais* met their supervisor for reorientation and discussion.

Aseea revealed that she sometimes gets from her patients things like oil, rice, vegetables or a meal. However she expressed concern that these days people are unwilling to pay, saying the *dais* already get paid for their job and should not be paid twice.

INDIA
How Caste Affects Indian Christians

The reality of caste continues to be a divisive factor in Indian society. The life and witness of the Christian community are affected as well. In this section, three perspectives on the caste system are outlined.

Since its founding in 1957, the Christian Institute for the Study of Religion and Society (CISRS) has sought the ultimate liberation of India's people, conscientiously bringing together people of different faiths, ideologies and traditions and analyzing Indian reality so that ways can be found to bring about the "radical restructuring of Indian society." In an unpublished manuscript titled, "Historical and Theological Tradition of Christianity in India," Richard W. Taylor of the CISRS staff gives the following overview of the socio-economic and cultural setting of India's caste system.

India is by no means an underdeveloped country. It is an extraordinarily poor, but quite developed country. . . . The middle class expands in size and comforts. But in a population of about seven hundred million, about half are below a very low poverty line. [Few, if any] Indian economists of any school . . . could imagine how to change this proportion by very much—give or take, say, fifty million. The green revolution has enabled India to grow much more rice and wheat than before in a truly remarkable way. But it has not, in general, bettered the income nor the diet of the poor.

But for India, economic class is probably not as important as caste is in keeping people in their place. Membership in some caste or other, high or low, is wholly hereditary. Encapsulation in groups hierarchically inter-related seems fundamental to the social fabric of India. Recently, a study tour of seminarians and younger clergy from Indianapolis visited [India]. After hearing from CISRS staff about their work of being of help in the struggle of untouchables to better their lot—in society as well as in churches—these young Americans testified . . . that all they had to do was purge their own prejudices, as the Americans had done in their own racial situation. I think this is arrogant nonsense because the very basic

Indian culture and religious presuppositions sanction, nay, even require caste.

There are five major caste groupings. All of these five major groupings contain differentials within themselves. At the top come the *brahmins*, who are traditionally learned and from whom all proper mainline priests come. Next come the warriors, including, historically, most rulers. Then come the tradespeople, including those in business. These three major groupings are known as "twice-born" castes because their young males undergo initiation rites.

The next group is very large, being made up of all of the other "clean" but subordinate castes of artisans, agriculturalists and laborers. These are called *sudras*.

Then come the fifth and bottom group of "unclean" untouchables. They make up about fifteen percent of the total population of India. They are sometimes called *harijans*—a Gandhian word meaning children of God. These are sometimes called scheduled castes because their castes are listed in a schedule incorporated in the Constitution of India in order to assure them of preferential consideration in education and employment. The activists among them sometimes call themselves *dalits*, which might be translated as "the poor".

Formal features of caste are that one does not marry nor dine nor even touch those of a different caste—especially those of a lower caste. There continues to be great exploitation of the untouchables. But different untouchable castes exclude each other just as they are excluded by higher caste people. Caste realities continue in the churches. In some areas where Christians have come from two different untouchable castes there is still little or no marriage between them—let alone intermarriage with Christians of other caste backgrounds. In other regions, Christians of a particular *sudra* caste background may dominate a church and its institutions, becoming bishops, principals and superintendents who are seen as giving the best jobs under their control to their own caste people to the detriment of . . . [other] Christians of outcaste background.

To "get ahead" in the Indian world today, three things are most helpful: high caste origin; English education; and money. The untouchable poor have none of these. Many of the elite English medium schools are church-related. While questions are asked about this, very few changes have been made.

In addition to the five major groups in the caste system there is a sixth major group in Indian society. This is made up of non-Hindu tribals who comprise many different tribes, languages and racial strains. The tribes tend to be in the hills and forests. Usually they are isolated with an area pretty much to themselves. In general, they have been treated as being very much beneath all "clean" caste people. Tribals make up about seven percent of the population of India. A good many of the tribes are largely Christian. Most tribals, like untouchables, are constitutionally assured of preferential consideration for education and employment.

Politically, India started in 1947 with a parliamentary democracy and great optimism. [It was] a democratic socialism with a mixed economy in which basic industry was in the public sector. The forms are little changed today, but because the high goals of economic well-being and social justice for all have not been reached, a certain disenchantment has set in.

* * *

At the Jubilee Convention of the CISRS, held in 1983, Brindavan C. Moses, an assistant director of CISRS, presented a paper titled: "Study and Action: Caste-Class Issue and CISRS Perspective." Some of his main points are presented here for reflection:

. . . how does one explain the immense hold of religion and caste on the lives of millions of Indians? How does one understand the question of the tribals' quest for self-identity, the "nationality" question, the "Aryan-Dravidian" difference, etc.?

With the deepening of the political and economic crises in India, the people who are affected by these are forced to organize themselves. . . . But, the tendency among the people has been . . . to organize themselves on communal, caste or ethnic lines . . .

. . . Caste is a major factor in social development. . . . the precise identification of classes [or castes] in Indian society has been very elusive . . . and is . . . complicated by the Hindu religious sanctions and prohibitions specific to Indian society. Such religious sanctions and prohibitions have been carried over by converts to Christianity and other religions and practiced with the same zeal and rigor. So, what needs to be studied and understood is:

- how profoundly caste has affected the process of change;
- whether caste has been conveniently used by the ruling classes and power elites to perpetuate underdevelopment of the majority, . . . to protect the gains of "development" by the few;
- whether caste has been used in a positive sense by the oppressed and exploited people to revolt against the oppressors and to assert their rights.

. . . The Indian church, unfortunately, is only a microcosm of the evil of the caste-class oppression and struggles of the country's unfolding history. But the church seems neither prepared nor willing to tackle this menace of caste-class oppression, despite the fact that the bulk of the Indian church is drawn from the weakest sections of Indian society.

To fully grasp the Indian social reality, one has to understand the phenomenon of caste and religion and the hold both have on the lives of the people, and also the ideology of caste and religion used effectively by the ruling classes and power elites for their self-interest. Caste ideology is deeply entrenched in the minds of Indians. In other words, caste, in the value system of a predominantly Hindu society, is almost an autonomous and independent variable.

To sum up, a small group of people or groups of people in Indian society use either caste or religion or both to further their power interests. Primordial loyalty to caste or loyalty to one's religion provides power bases for political mobilization and support in India. In the same way, the oppressed also use caste and/or religious symbols to rally the people to fight for their rights.

* * *

The Kottayam Group from the State of Kerala, in preparing for the World Council of Churches Sixth Assembly in 1983, prepared a statement on caste titled, "Caste That Kills the Life of the Community," by Dr. K.V. Mathew, from which the following paragraphs are excerpted.

. . . Caste is associated with work. "Barber" is a caste, "carpenter" is another, "scavenger" is yet another. The upper-caste community develops an attitude of distaste towards people who are engaged in professions which are regarded by the upper-class as *melecha*— despicable. The upper-class thus widens the gulf between the high and the low in society.

Of course, casteism is strong among the Hindus. But what about Christians, among whom, theoretically, caste distinction does not exist? A sociological analysis would reveal facts which would bring surprises to many in the church. Caste does exist in the Christian church. It is true. How do we know it?

A recent survey [1981] taken by a commission appointed by the Mar Thoma Church brought forth the following facts:

1. The Christians of Kerala consider the newly-converted Christians as low-caste. Their social contact with converted Christians is meager. The Syrian Christians consider themselves as belonging to the upper-caste, the Brahmins. Although they have been Christians for centuries, the caste feelings haven't changed—even today.

2. The caste Christians [meaning of "lower" caste] are provided with separate centers of worship. The older Christians seldom worship along with them. The younger generation of the Syrian Christians have developed a more positive attitude, so far

as worship with the caste Christians is concerned. However they, too, may hesitate to enter into marriage alliances with them. These poor Christians, now due to the impact of Marxism,* have developed a sense of self-respect and pride for their own ancient culture and traditions. They now prefer to stand alone without the Syrian Christians. They understand that this will provide them with better opportunities for development. These congregations are being recognized as parishes by the Mar Thoma church. The church gives particular attention to their development.

3. For centuries, these people were slaves and were under bonded labor. Consequently, during this long period of slavery, they developed a sense of inferiority. They have been made morbid. As a result they cannot compete with people who enjoy freedom in life . . .

4. However, we see life among them. They are hard-working and blessed with artistic talents, music, dancing, painting, etc. If encouraged they can, no doubt, compete with others.

5. Caste brought with it prejudices. Even if the caste Christians come up in life, the prejudice of the upper-caste remains. A positive response towards the "low-caste" Christians is yet to grow among the upper-class Christians. An attitude developed through centuries cannot easily be annulled.

6. Caste also brings with it color prejudices—the black complexion and the physical features are not appreciated by Christians who belong to another race. The converts probably come from the Negroid racial background [while] the brown-colored older Christians come from the Dravidian group. The incompatibilities among them are many, the upper-class would say. So they hesitate to have social intercourse with them.

None of these objections or prejudices stand in the life of a Christian social perspective. A basic change of attitude on the part of [all] is necessary to change the situation, i.e., a new life in Christ alone would cut the ice. . . . [Each] needs to stand before the Lord and acknowledge one another as brothers and sisters in Christ. This sentence is easy to write, but very hard to make a reality. The death of caste-color prejudices would lead to life in Christ. Bearing of the Cross is inevitable. One has to bear the Cross patiently, which leads to death and new life.

*The state of Kerala had elected a Marxist government, which lost a subsequent election.

Christ Confronts India
by B.V. Subbamma

. . . Christianity has hardly touched and hardly makes an impact on the great religions of India. This is a great challenge for the church today. . . . There is a definite need for rethinking Christianity in terms which would be intelligible to the Indian mind. Christianity's foreignness in the cultural sense of the word has to be overcome, i.e. it must become "at home" in India against the background of Indian culture without the danger of compromising its fundamental truths.

. . . There is a great need for change of church structure. . . . [but] Indian Christians are very slow to accept and in some cases are opposed to indigenous experiments. While this might be the state of the church, what of the non-Christians in India who constitute over 97 percent of the total population of the country? It is encouraging to know from several sources that they have a healthy attitude towards Christ, but they are anxious to receive him in an Indian garb.

It is high time that we should change and introduce indigenous methods both in the existing church and to communicate the Gospel to non-Christians and thus establish "indigenous churches."[2]

Miss Subbamma, an evangelist and educator, advocates a deep level of cultural adaptation for Christianity in India. This selection is from her book, Christ Confronts India *(Madras: The Diocesan Press, 1973).*

We Betrayed the Poor
By Mathai Zachariah

We betrayed the poor—we, the elite.
We, the fifteen out of every hundred,
Rose by ascending spirals to giddy heights,
While they, the eighty-five in every hundred,
Remained on earth, hungry.
We, the intelligentsia, betrayed the poor, for thirty long years.
We slept, hibernated, while they toiled.
We thought only of the towel and the basin
And never of the toils of the revolutionary.
We failed to see their bleeding points.
We, the intellectuals, betrayed the cause.
We tasted of the joys of life,
Amidst their joyless world of sweat and blood.
We planned, but no one planned the planners.
Our ideologies, our paths—
Sarvodaya, Socialism, Secularism, Swatantra
We forgot that ideologies are anthropologies—
hopes about [humankind's] nature and destiny.
We are nothing but hypocrites—cowards all,
Who call for sacrifice and selfless service, save for ourselves!
So again we are on square one,
To start the pilgrimage again.
Rich with hopes, heavy with anxieties
Carrying with us the load of promises and threats.
"A journey of a thousand miles begins with the first step",
Make this the first step, Lord,
And help us to grasp the moment.
For your sake
And for the sake of six-hundred million of your people.

Mathai Zachariah is general secretary of the National Council of Churches of India.

The Mission of the Cross
By M. Azariah

Right from my teen age when I first read about the great Sadhu
Sundar Singh, I have come to believe in the mission of the cross
as most appropriate for India. This idea was brought home to me
in one of the most telling episodes from the life of the Sadhu.

He writes about an occasion when he was travelling through the
snowclad Himalayan ranges across to Tibet. It was heavily snowing
on this particular day. A Tibetan Lama (monk) had joined him on
his way and also in conversation. Before long they came upon a
heap of snow with a piece of saffron cloth peeping out. Quickly
they cleared the snow and found a monk trapped under the snow
and he was unconscious. The Sadhu and the Lama still had a few
miles to walk before reaching the next village. Unless they ran fast
they might not save their own lives, said the Lama. But the Sadhu
insisted on carrying the unconscious monk to safety. The Lama
counselled the Sadhu to leave the monk alone and run for life lest
all three die on the way. The Sadhu said he could not do this as
the spirit of Christ in him constrained him to carry the monk with
him. But the Lama scoffed at the "unwise" Sadhu and ran away
to save his own life.

The Sadhu carried his precious load, moving in slow steps. Soon
he found himself quite warmed up in body contact with the monk.
After walking for about a mile the monk regained consciousness
and enough strength for himself to walk along with the Sadhu.
Then after clearing another mile in the snow, not far away from a
village, these two found a heap of snow freshly formed. On opening it they found that the Lama, who had parted their company
not long ago, was now caught under the snow. Turning him around
they found him dead. It was then, the Sadhu says, he understood
the meaning of the words of the Master: "He who would lose his
life for my sake will gain it but he who wants to save his life will
lose it." (Luke 9:24). And herein is the way of the cross for our
mission.

*The Rev. M. Azariah is general secretary of the Church of South India.
This is taken from his book,* Witnessing in India Today *(Madras: United
Evangelical Lutheran Churches, 1983).*

SRI LANKA
Unfulfilled Promises

The suffering of tea plantation workers in Sri Lanka and their cries for justice need to be heard around the world. Tamil-speaking Hindu workers were first recruited from India by the British in the 19th century. For generations, they lived separate from a population made up mainly of Buddhist Sinhalese, but also lived apart from the island's indigenous Tamils in the north and east. When Ceylon (Sri Lanka) was granted independence in 1948, this Tamil community of recent Indian origin was disenfranchised; most were deemed "stateless", and despite subsequent Indo-Ceylon agreements, many remained so.

The entire nation has suffered heavily as a result of recent racial violence: 150,000 jobs have been lost; 17 major manufacturing plants are in ruin; foreign investment has been affected in the climate of instability; greater power has been given to armed forces and police to implement the ban on the Tamil United Liberation Front. Amid all this, the writings of Tamil tea plantation workers reveal a depth of consciousness that underscores the vulnerability and suffering they in particular have long endured. Note that this and other poems like it have been translated into Sinhala, an historic effort of communication.

We Must Leave, We Know Not Why
by Kurinji Nathan

We cleared forest and hard rocks broke,
All through our life, back-breaking work;
Today we leave, today we go,
To face what loneliness we don't know.

We gathered wealth for this land's gain,
Accepted hardships, did not complain.
The little we've found is on this land
But all that we must leave behind.

Unkind names we were always called,
"Illegitimate" was cruelly hurled;
Today we leave to shed our blood,
No word spoken we leave here dumb.

We toiled and earned with self-respect,
With all this strain our spirits bent;
We are broken beings, maimed we go,
Driven out, no justice to show.

Poem from For the Dawning of the New, *edited by Jeffrey Abayasekera and D. Preman Niles, published by the Commission of Theological Concerns of the Christian Conference of Asia. Kurinji Nathan, a child of tea plantation workers, teaches in a plantation school.*

Our flesh and blood is in this soil,
Here we have buried our kin and toil,
Now we go with no strength to stand,
Eyes filling with tears for an unknown land.

Following a dialogue with Sri Lankan Tamils and Sinhalese, members of the Southern Asia Working Group of the National Council of the Churches of Christ in the USA sought to clarify their thinking and, at the same time, give guidance to U.S. churches on ways to promote justice and reconciliation for the people of this troubled nation. The resulting statement, excerpted here, is offered in the belief that churches in North America need to be sensitive to the dynamics that are polarizing Tamils and Sinhalese, including those of the Christian faith. Both Protestant and Catholic churches in Sri Lanka are trying to build bridges across the divisions that separate the two communities. Churches are, in fact, the only religious groups that include both Tamils and Sinhalese.

There are ways in which people in local churches in the U.S. and Canada can touch the Sri Lankan crisis. One is by supporting their denominational officials when they urge their government to take certain actions with regard to Sri Lanka. Others can get to know some of the many Sri Lankans who live in North America.* Those who travel to Sri Lanka (one of southern Asia's most popular tourist spots) may prepare themselves by studying the current situation there.

The repercussions of the polarity between Sri Lankan Tamils and Sinhalese will not fade soon. Because of this, it is crucial that North American Christians grow in awareness of the situation and continue to pray for those caught up in it.

Resolution on Sri Lanka

The breakdown of order, the well-documented violations of human rights by government officials, the spiraling mistrust of those in authority due to broken agreements, the seemingly increased commitment of the government to a military solution of the problem, all compound despair for Sri Lankans at home and abroad. In this situation, guarantees for the survival of the Tamil people and for the stability and well being of both the Sinhala and Tamil communities become urgent priorities.

The NCCC/USA has, in consultation with the National Christian Council of Sri Lanka and in cooperation with the World Council of Churches and the Christian Conference of Asia, contributed to

---

*Trust the Spirit, Share the Struggle, the leaders' guide to this study, offers ideas on how to involve a southern Asian visitor in a group's study plan. The NCC's Task Force on Militarization in Asia and the Pacific, which developed the filmstrip *Dangerous Crossroads* (see inside back cover) can provide names of speakers knowledgeable on the Sri Lanka crisis.

programs seeking justice and peace for the troubled people of Sri Lanka. We have become convinced that the following additional steps must be taken by the Churches in North America as part of the international ecumenical response to this critical situation.

1. We urge the immediate cessation of violence by all parties.

2. We urge the Government of Sri Lanka to give courageous and vigorous political leadership by taking new initiatives for peace and reconciliation and thus affirm that it is the government of the whole nation and not only of the majority community.

3. We urge the Government of Sri Lanka to provide protection without distinction for all citizens of the nation who are threatened by violence; to safeguard the human rights of all people in accordance with accepted international norms; and to facilitate the provisions of aid to the homeless, the dispossessed, and the families of those who have been killed, have disappeared, or are in detention. To this end, we urge access be given to the predominantly Tamil areas of Sri Lanka by independent observers, church persons, relief organizations and particularly the International Committee of the Red Cross.

4. We urge the Goverment of the USA to take initiatives in developing concerted international action to seek: (1) the end of reprisals by the police and security forces in Sri Lanka; (2) the termination of the Prevention of Terrorism Act; and (3) the restoration of full judicial process.

5. We call upon all governments, especially those of the United States and India to refrain from providing any form of military or security assistance to the parties in conflict which can only worsen the situation and delay a solution.

6. We urge the religious leadership in Sri Lanka—Buddhist, Hindu, Muslim and Christian, building on their years of experience with interreligious dialogue and cooperation, to seek new means of reconciliation, and to request the Asia section of the World Conference on Religion and Peace to take steps to support such a process.

7. We call upon the governments of the United States and Europe to grant refugee status to those Tamils who have sought safe haven outside Sri Lanka for legitimate political reasons and in no case to forcibly repatriate them.

8. We call for prayer for the churches and for peace and justice for all the people of Sri Lanka, and pledge our cooperation in efforts of reconciliation between the Tamil and Sinhala communities, and offer our resources to minister to the many human needs caused by this tragic violence.

Adopted by the NCCC
Governing Board, May 1985

PAKISTAN
Missionary Work in the Modern World
by Antony Fernando

Not long ago it was maintained that a Christian's study of another religion would be harmful to one's faith. Any religion outside Christianity was considered "pagan" and contact with "paganism" was carefully to be avoided.

That extreme view does not prevail any longer. But the old Christian unconcern for other religions and philosophies is not totally dead. For many, the study of another religion, even though not so harmful, is not a necessity. At best, it is a good pastime for those who have a surplus of time on their hands.

Alfred North Whitehead, in *Religion in the Making* (New American Library, 1974) says:

> The decay of Christianity and Buddhism, as determinative influences in modern thought, is partly due to the fact that each religion has unduly sheltered itself from the other. The self-sufficient pedantry of learning and the confidence of ignorant zealots have combined to shut up each religion in its own forms of thought. Instead of looking to each other for deeper meanings, they have remained self-satisfied and unfertilized.

To understand the thought of the founder of a religion fully, one has also to discover why [such a doctrine was taught]. The aim that a particular religious founder strived to attain is as important for the understanding of the religion as the teaching itself. It is because [the founder] had a particular aim that one particular doctrine was taught rather than another. Particularly for a Christian student, who has the additional interest of comparing [Christianity] with Buddhism, its *why* is as important as its *what*.

To see a religion in terms of its *why* is naturally to see it in terms of its primary function, or better, its mission. If there is an affinity between Christianity and Buddhism with regard to their mission, then an important question is bound to arise with regard to the fulfillment of that mission, or in other words, with regard to missionary work. What is the responsibility of the Christian missionary

From *Antony Fernando*, Buddhism and Christianity—Their Inner Affinity, *(Colombo: Ecumenical Institute for Study and Dialogue, 1981).*

who comes to realize that there could be an affinity between his or her work and that of the Buddhist missionary, [since] both Buddhism and Christianity are missionary religions?

This is a question that should not be sidetracked at the end of a study of Buddhism. . . . It may, further, not be safe to leave such a question unexplored, especially because Christianity itself at this moment is passing through a stage of uncertainty as to the relevance of its own missionary role. There are many Christians today who are beginning to ask [whether] missionary work or the making of converts could serve any purpose in contemporary society.

Strange as it may sound, the study of Buddhism, instead of undermining the position of the Christian, could rather enhance it by bringing . . . a new realization of the contemporary relevance of mission. For that, of course, one has first to understand in its correct sense the reality implied by convert work. Missionary work could naturally not serve any valid purpose in the modern world if it is taken in the misconstrued sense of converting or bringing people from one religion to another. The purpose of missionary work is not to bring people to a new institution or a new religion. It is, rather, to bring an individual from a state of mental childishness to a state of mental adulthood. The work of the missionary is the work of helping people to be adults, technically called *arahats* in Buddhism and in Christianity, saints.

If missionary work is seen in that perspective, its importance and its relevance to modern society become self-evident. If the end of missionary work is personality-transformation then there has probably been no era in the history of humankind in which it was more urgently needed than today. Purely from the side of the world's population, there has never been such a great number needing education in personality-upliftment.

But for missionary work of that type to be effective, the missionary, . . . Buddhist or Christian, has to be equipped with an enlarged vision. A missionary

- can no longer afford to be insular in approaching religious truths;
- cannot claim to have the total monopoly over the truth of an individual's path to spiritual nobility;
- must be prepared to admit that if he or she has [a] technique for personality-upliftment, that others too may have theirs.

Therefore a Christian need not have to compete with the Buddhist . . . [but] rather collaborate . . . Missionary work or the work of educating human beings to adulthood is a task that Christians and Buddhists can labor at hand in hand. Even the very extensiveness of the task in the contemporary world would justify such a collaboration.

[A person's] growth to full "humanhood" was more important to Christ than the religious system or the institution. That is why Christ opposed the attitude of Jewish priests who tried to enslave humankind by religion. That is what he boldly insinuated when he declared; "The Sabbath is for human beings and not human beings for the Sabbath. . . ."

The Buddha expressed the same idea when he compared religion to a raft which carries travellers from one shore to another. Once the shore is reached, he said, the traveller should not carry the raft on the head!

Thus for both the Buddha and Christ, what mattered in reality was the mission of the religion and not religion as such. If that was the view of the founders of the two religions, would it be right for their followers to accept another? And finally, in case there is an affinity between the two religions with regard to their mission, would it not be more in keeping the the desires of the two founders that their missionaries collaborate in the execution of this vital mission?

The modern Christian missionary should not be taken aback if as a result of such collaboration [there would be one day be] individuals who, after successfully benefitting from the technique of both religions, would want to consider themselves Buddhist-Christians or Christian-Buddhists. It is quite possible that as forms of personality-upliftment the two systems have elements that are complementary to each other. It could well be that modern humankind needs both a peace of mind and a self-fulfillment achieved through an active commitment to society's development; both a sense of self-dependence and a sense of relationship; both a life of self-control and a correctly-oriented emotional life.

The likelihood of individuals profitting from both systems is thus not an impossibility. If such a development takes place, neither the Buddhist nor the Christian has a right to object to it, for the Buddha is not the exclusive monopoly of the Buddhists, nor Christ of the Christians.

Such an eventuality will not disturb a Christian who has understood religion and its function in the way that Christ understood it. For Christ, religion was not an end in itself. This is a point that is often overlooked, but which a modern Christian missionary will do well to remember.

Poems from Pakistan
by Nazir Qaiser

These poems were written in Urdu, the national language of Pakistan, by a Pakistani Christian poet. In "Poem for a Bleak Season," the poet expresses his faith in the ultimate triumph of truth and justice over all tyranny and oppression. Nature constantly gives evidence for hope, and these natural signs are a promise of certain liberation. The anthem reveals Christ as the source of the poet's determination and courage. The Christian community sings in order to root itself in the power of its Lord and to commit itself to the spreading of the Lord's kingdom in this miserable, struggling world. Justice, truth and love will prevail in Christ.

POEM FOR A BLEAK SEASON

Who can confine
   the paths of fragrance
   with barbed wire?

Who can cut
   the unfolding fingers of dawn
   with daggers?

The morning cannot hide
   behind a fortification of clouds
On every wounded branch
   flowers are about to bloom.
Lips move
   even on the face of silence.

ANTHEM

This is our vow—
   to make the stranger our own—
   we're the lovers of Life.
This is our vow.
The flames of tyranny
   we'll turn into roses.
The waves of the storm
   we'll harness as oars.
Christ is our helmsman;
   He, too, is the shore.
We're the lovers of Life.
This is our vow.
In eyes long vacant
   we'll ignite fresh dreams.
Through the windows of the night
   we'll shine a new moon.
The One we accompany
   is the Star of the Morning.
We're the lovers of Life.
This is our vow.
This is our vow.

_____

Translated and introduced by Kristine Rogers.

NOTES

Diverted Streams of History

No Longer a Bird with Clipped Wings

1. Jonathan Lindell, *Nepal and the Gospel of God* (United Mission to Nepal, in collaboration with Masihi Sahitya Sanstha, 1979), p. 41.
2. Lindell, p. 42.
3. Lindell, p. 213.
4. Norma Kehrberg, "Nepali Songs: Personal Perspective of Two Contemporary Artists." Unpublished manuscript.
5. Lindell, p. 208.

Faith Streams

Christ in Indian Thought: A Dialogue

1. Richard W. Taylor, "The Historical and Theological Tradition of Christianity in India," unpublished chapter for inclusion in a forthcoming Christian Conference of Asia publication.
2. S. Radhakrishnan, in *Philosophy of Sarvepalli Radhakrishnan*, ed. P.A. Schilpp, 1952, pp. 103, 121, 122.
3. M.M. Thomas, "The Christological Task in India," in *Religion and Society, The First Twenty-Five Years (1953–1978)*, ed. Richard W. Taylor (Madras: Christian Literature Society for CIRS, 1982), Vol XI, No. 3, Sept. 1964.
4. M.M. Thomas, "Editorial" in *Religion and Society*, Vol. XVI, No. 2, June 1969, p. 206.
5. David Kopf, *The Brahmo Samaj and the Shaping of the Modern Indian Mind*, (Princeton, NJ: Princeton University Press, 1979).
6. Taylor, "The Historical and Theological Tradition of Christianity in India."
7. Richard W. Taylor, *Jesus in Indian Paintings*, (Madras: CISRS/CLS, 1975), pp. 59 ff.
8. Taylor, "The Historical and Theological Tradition of Christianity in India."
9. Taylor, *Jesus in Indian Paintings*.
10. Thomas, *Religion and Society, op.cit.*
11. V. Chakkarai, *Jesus the Avatar*, (Madras: CLS., 1930,), p. 123.
12. Taylor, "The Historical and Theological Tradition of Christianity in India".
13. Thomas, *Religion and Society, op.cit.*
14. D.A. Thangasamy, "Views of Some Christian Thinkers in India on Conversion and Baptism," in *Religion and Society*, Vol XIX, No. 1, March 1972, pp. 266 and 281.

15. Thangasamy.
16. Taylor, "The Historical and Theological Tradition of Christianity in India".
17. P.D. Sham Rao, "The Church in a Pluralistic Society," in *Krisht Vidya*, A Quarterly Journal of the Christian Retreat and Study Center, Rajpur, Dehra Dun, U.P. Vol. 3, No. 2, June 1983. pp. 15 ff.
18. Taylor, "The Historical and Theological Tradition of Christianity in India".
19. Rao.
20. S.J. Amaldoss, "Ashrams and Social Justice," a paper written for the Interdisciplinary Research Seminar on the Indian Church in the Struggle for a New Society, Bangalore, October, 1981.
21. Rao.
22. Thangasamy.
23. Thangasamy.

The Church Today in Bangladesh

1. *Pro Mundi Vita: Dossiers*, "Bangladesh: A Test Case for a Self-Reliant Nation and a Church," (Brussels: August 1979).
2. A. L'Imperio, *Statistics of Bangladesh, the Country and the Church,* (Dinapur: Unique Press and Mukul Press, 1978), pp. 25, 26.
3. M. Kalathil, *Vidyajyoyi*, "Harijans and Conversions: Another Point of View," 1978, pp. 12–17.
4. *Pro Mundi Vita: Dossiers*, p. 46.

Militarization, Justice and Peace

A Young Person's View of Militarization

1. *Oppressor and Victim*, (Singapore: Christian Conference of Asia Youth, 1983), Preamble.
2. *Ibid.*, Introduction.
3. "Youth Program Committee", published by Christian Conference of Asia Youth for a conference held in Doi Suthep, Thailand, 1982. p. 2.
4. *Ibid.*, p. 2.
5. *Ibid.*, p. 3.
6. *Ibid.*, p. 3.
7. *Oppressor and Victim, op.cit.*, pp. 131–133.
8. *Ibid.*
9. *Ibid.* p. 156.

APPENDIX I

Three living faiths of southern Asia:
Hinduism, Buddhism and Islam

Hinduism

Hinduism is a container into which the ideas and experiences of the teeming Indian subcontinent have been pouring for five thousand years. (The word "Hindu" comes from the great river Indus, in what is now Pakistan, along which Indian civilization began about 3000 B.C.)

[The key ideas of Hinduism] are expressed in many different ways,   but they hang together with a subtle logic. Let us follow the thread of these ideas, marking our progress with seven knots in the string.

Dharma

The Indian word for religion is *dharma*. But *dharma* means something more like "duty" than like "religion" in our sense. . . . *Dharma* is not a set of general rules, like the Ten Commandments, but a varying prescription for each individual according to his [or her] age, family position, sex, education, and the like.

In the *Bhagavad-Gita*, most important of the Hindu scriptures, the god Vishnu appears to Arjuna the warrior, who is paralyzed by moral scruples. He shrinks from the suffering and death he is about to inflict. But Vishnu urges him to fight. As a member of the warrior caste, it is his duty. To leave the battle would be more than a disgrace; it would be a sin.[1]

Mahatma Gandhi, though a pacifist, endorsed this teaching. In favor of obedience to caste duty he wrote: "Why should we choose to claim as individuals the right during this present brief life-period to break through all the conventions wherein we were placed at birth by God Himself?"[2]

Samasara

Acceptance of an inferior or a distasteful *dharma* is made easier by a second fundamental Hindu idea. *Samsara* (reincarnation) is the belief that the soul is born and reborn over and over again, on different level of existence . . .

So . . . Vishnu tells Arjuna, he need not be unduly concerned about those he will slay. Death is certain for the living; rebirth certain for the dead. His slaying makes no great difference.[3] Even Mahatma Gandhi defended the caste system on the same basis. . . .

This conviction . . . is strange to most [North] Americans. Yet it is the common belief of much of Asia. Along with it goes another conviction about the way these successive lives are linked together.

Karma

Karma is the word for that linkage. It means literally "action.". . . Our actions in past lives have created the conditions under which we live now. Our present actions determine our future. By doing good today, we may be reborn . . . as a Brahman . . . But thieving and lust will create a future life as a rat or a goat.

Atman

Lives come and go, strung like beads on the thread of *karma*. But in all this flux and change, there is something in every person that endures. . . . The most famous

---

Excerpts on Hinduism and Buddhism from When Faith Meets Faith, *by David M. Stowe (New York: Friendship Press, 1963, rev. 1981). The section on Islam is excerpted from an unpublished paper by Dr. Byron L. Haines of the Office on Christian-Muslim Relations of the National Council of the Churches of Christ.*

expression of this conviction is found in an ancient scripture, the *Chandogya Un-panishad.* "That which is the finest essence—this whole world has that as its Self. That is Reality. That is Atman. That art thou." Self and the Godhead, *atman* and *Brahman,* the soul of the individual and the Soul of the universe: these are really identical.

Maya

Hinduism has a word for the changing experience of the obvious and superficial "me," my "personality." The word is *maya,* which has the same root as our word "magic."

. . . [The] events of everyday life—and of world history, too—are a kind of mirage. [They] come and go—and nothing has really happened so far as reality—the *atman,* the self—is concerned.

Moksha

. . . *Moksha* stands for a blessed permanent exit from the cycle of rebirth. It is release from the intolerable dreariness of participation in the world of *maya,* the never-ending play of illusions . . . *Moksha* is the goal of Hinduism, its term for salvation.

Since it must be completely different from anything that happens in the *maya* world of ordinary experience, *moksha* is difficult to describe. Probably the closest parallel is found in the experience of deep, dreamless sleep. "In this state a father is no father, a mother is no mother, the worlds are no worlds, the Vedas [scriptures] no Vedas . . ."[4]

Yogas

. . . *Yoga,* from the same root as "yoke," suggests the discipline that is required to break the chain of *karma,* the law that binds one to a never-ending series of rebirths.

Hindu Ethics

. . . Christians—and Westerners in general—are accustomed to judging the value of religion by its ethical results . . . Let us look . . . then, at the moral emphases that are part of Hinduism . . . Gandhi's rules for his ashram or community of disciples provide an interesting summary . . .

● *a vow of truth*

. . . Central to truth as Gandhi understood it is *ahimsa,* which literally means noninjury. Gandhi believed firmly that *ahimsa* represents tremendous force. He called it *satyagraha,* literally "power of truth," and depended upon this moral power of nonviolent goodwill for practical social reform. The winning of Indian independence from Britain is usually credited to this strategy of Gandhi's . . .

● *a vow of celibacy*

All physical desire must be renounced, even in marriage. Relationships should be purely spiritual.

● *a vow of control of appetite*

All stimulating and exciting seasonings that do not add to food value but simply please the appetite are a hindrance to ethical living.

● *a vow of nonthieving*

This is very broadly interpreted to mean living on a bare subsistence level, using nothing that is not essential . . .

● *a vow of nonpossession*

This means giving away all one's surplus until the standards of the poorest have been raised.

● *a vow of* swadeshi *or "buy at home"*

. . . each person and each group should be self-sustaining and continue in an accustomed way of life. It is wrong to seek artificial luxury through widespread trade and a cosmopolitan culture.

● *a vow of fearlessness*

"There is only One whom we have to fear, that is God."

- *a vow against untouchability*

Although Gandhi defended the caste system, he fought against the degrading of outcastes . . .

- *a vow of khaddar or labor*

Every Gandhian was expected to do some manual work daily to testify to the dignity of labor . . .

Most items on this list quite clearly belong to the Hindu heritage. Others, however, come from elsewhere. The concern with social reform, the interpretation of *ahimsa* in a positive sense as universal love, the affirmation of human dignity in the outcaste and in labor, the "fear of God". . . come rather from the West with its Christian social tradition.

. . . It was the New Testament that confirmed Gandhi's belief in nonviolent resistance. He wrote, "When I read in the Sermon on the Mount such passages as . . .'Love your enemies; pray for them that persecute you, that ye may be sons of your Father which is in heaven,' I was simply overjoyed."[5]

NOTES

1. *Bhagavad-Gita*, trans. Swami Prabhavananda and Christopher Isherwood (New York: Mentor Books, 1954 [by permission of Marcel Rodd, orig. publisher]), pp. 38ff.
2. C.F. Andrews, *Mahatma Gandhi's Ideas* (London: George Allen and Unwin, Ltd., 1929), p. 129.
3. *Bhagavad-Gita*, pp. 38ff.
4. Based on Swami Nikhilananda's *Hinduism: Its Meaning for the Liberation of the Spirit* (New York: Harper & Brothers, 1958), p. 45.
5. Andrews, op.cit., p. 192.

Buddhism

Of all the human beings who ever lived, Buddha is probably the one most like Jesus of Nazareth in his influence upon history. Gautama was born not in a stable but in a palace, near the border between present-day northern India and Nepal. His father surrounded him with sensual pleasures and material comforts in order to insulate him from the sorrows, frustrations and pains of [human]kind.

In his twenties, however, Prince Gautama did discover these bitter realities. Legend tells of his accidental meetings with a senile man, a desperately sick man . . . and a corpse being carried to the funeral pyre. Thus he learned that the vigor and enjoyments of the body last only a few years; that even in those years [human beings are] subject to pain and disease; and that at the end death comes to everyone. Brooding on these discoveries, he encountered a Sadhu, a Hindu holy man. From him he learned that it is possible to leave the futile world of sensual desires and enjoyments and to seek an abiding peace and satisfaction. That night he kissed his infant son and his sleeping wife goodbye and went out to seek that peace.

For seven years his search took the forms traditional in Hinduism of that time and place. He practiced *yoga* and speculated philosophically on the cosmos, the One and the soul . . . But it was all in vain, for no transforming insight came.

Then he remembered a happy experience of his youth. "I was seated under the cool shade of a rose-apple tree, and without sensual desires, without evil ideas, I attained and abode in the first trance of joy and pleasure arising from seclusion and combined with reasoning and investigation. Perhaps this is the way to Enlightment." he thought.[1] And so there arose his great idea of the Middle Way . . .

Having gotten his sence of direction, Gautama seated himself under a spreading tree near Gaya in northeastern India and began a long period of concentrated meditation. . . . Though tempted by demons, he maintained his vigilance and resolution. Finally, at the full moon of May, 544 B.C. . . . he entered into a vivid experience of "enlightenment" (*bodhi*). Henceforth, Gautama was to be called "Buddha," the Enlightened One.

. . . Gautama, reacting against the complexities of Hinduism, kept his message simple. He summarized it in Four Noble Truths.

● *Pain*. "Birth is painful, old age is painful, sickness is painful, death is painful, sorrow, lamentation, dejection and despair are painful. Contact with unpleasant things is painful, not getting what one wishes is painful."[2]

● *The cause of pain*. The cause of pain is "craving, which tends to rebirth [by creating *karma*] . . . the craving for passion, the craving for existence, the craving for nonexistence."

● *The cessation of pain*. Pain ceases with the absolute end of craving.

● *The way that leads to cessation of pain*. One achieves freedom from all craving by following the noble Eightfold Path:

1. RIGHT VIEWS. First of all comes a correct understanding of our problem, which understanding is expressed in the first three Noble Truths. . . .

2. RIGHT INTENTION. Correct understanding must not remain a merely theoretical or abstract thing. It must be translated into will, into an energetic striving to act upon truth.

3. RIGHT SPEECH. Words must correspond with our inner attitudes. . . .

4. RIGHT ACTION. These correspond in a sense to the Ten Commandments.[3] Do not kill; do not steal; do not commit any impurity; do not lie; do not use intoxicants.

5. RIGHT LIVELIHOOD. Obviously, you should not allow yourself to be drawn into an occupation—such as butchering, soldiering, or bartending—that would lead you into wrong action. The Buddhist ideal is the life of a monk or a nun. . .

6. RIGHT EFFORT . . . Evil thoughts are to be overcome, passions controlled. . . .

7. RIGHT MINDFULNESS OR ALERTNESS. By this Gautama meant primarily a habit of constant, cool, objective analysis of the real situation. For example, if you are plagued with desire for bodily pleasures, go out to the field where the corpses are burned. As you look at the half-burned bodies and the disjointed bones, you can contemplate the body "as it really is," in life and in death. . . .

8. RIGHT CONCENTRATION. The crown of religious life is such absolute control of the mind that it remains completely focused upon truth. . . .

The Buddhist Goal

Nirvana corresponds to heaven in the Christian view of salvation but is even more difficult to describe. It originates in a negative idea: the absence of all that is unpleasant, raised to an infinite degree! Nirvana, an Indian word, literally means "blowing out," as a candle flame is extinguished by a breath. . . .

. . . [Gautama Buddha's] practical spirit brought a welcome change from the jungle growth of Indian theological speculations. His preaching and his example constantly stressed sane moderation of thought and behavior. His message was a realistic attempt to deal with the sadness of a world in which flowers wither and death separates those who love.[4]

Southern Asian Buddhism

. . . In several southern Asian countries, Buddhism is so dominant that recent revivals of nationalism in [Sri Lanka], Burma, and Thailand have involved impressive Buddhist revivals also.

. . . Among well-educated southern Buddhists, Gautama's agnosticism and humanism persist. To them, devotional practices are simply exercises in spiritual self-cultivation . . . But for the average southern Buddhist . . . Buddha is a divine being resident in heaven.

100

. . . While southern Buddhism has been faithful to the practical and rational emphasis in Gautama's teaching, it may have neglected his essential spirit. He talked about calculated self-cultivation but exhibited an outgoing, self-giving spirit. This became the idea that dominated Buddhism as it went north.

Mahayana, or northern Buddhism, offers a hospitable way to salvation for all [people], whether or not they are capable of the spiritual feats of the Buddha himself.

. . . Perhaps the profoundest contribution of the Mahayana spirit is the *bodhisattva*, a saviour. For southern Buddhism the supreme figure is the *arahat*, he who has followed the Eightfold Path to the top of the mountain and achieved enlightenment. But what if the *arahat*, having achieved salvation for himself, should then of his own free will refuse nirvana and turn back into the world of suffering and rebirth in order to help others? Doing so he becomes a *bodhisattva*, "one whose being is enlightenment," a compassionate saviour.

. . . Basically, however, the *bodhisattva* belongs to a religious world radically different from that of the Christian Saviour. Even Mahayana Buddhism rests upon detachment from the illusions of existence. There is no ultimate difference between good and evil; nor is there any emphasis upon human sinfulness. . . .

Buddhist moral teaching springs from the conviction that, until we achieve salvation, we are bound up with all other living things in the beautiful but painful process of "existence." Out of this arises sympathy for our fellow creatures, a compassion like that so finely exemplified by Gautama. Moreover, the rule of *karma* ordains that good comes only from good. . . . To that law, that love, that *dharma*, the Buddhist is asked to give cheerful allegiance.

NOTES

1. Clarence H. Hamilton, *Buddhism* (New York: The Liberal Arts Press, 1952), p. 17.
2. E. A. Burtt, *The Teachings of the Compassionate Buddha* (New York: Mentor Books, 1955), p. 30.
3. There is also a Buddhist list of "Ten Immoral Actions": killing, stealing, unchastity, lying, slandering, harsh languages, frivolous talk, covetousness, ill will, and false views.
4. J.B. Pratt, *The Pilgrimage of Buddhism* (New York: The Macmillan Company, 1928), p. 22.

Islam

In spite of a long history of association, the church and most Christians have very little understanding of Islam and the Muslim world. Today this situation is not helped by the prejudice against and stereotypes of Islam and Muslims that appear regularly in the media's reporting of events in the Middle East. If Christians wish to be true to their own religious principles they must seek to understand as fully as possible the religion of Islam and the people who live by its tenets. . . .

At the heart of Islam is the worship of God. No other world religion is more concerned than Islam to give God His due in every aspect of human life. The Arabic word *Islam* means "submission." It is submission to the will of God, not because of obligations due God, nor because of a fear of God, but because the believer is thankful to God for the divine grace and mercy that has made life possible. The word *Muslim* designates the one who practices or is the doer of Islam. Muslims believe that the God (the Arabic word for God is *Allah*) whom they worship is the same God worshipped by Jews and Christians. It is the God of Abraham, the same God who has revealed himself through the prophets beginning with Adam and continuing through Moses, Jesus, and finally, Muhammad.

In speaking about God, Muslims use the phrase, "I bear witness that there is no God but God and that Muhammad is his messenger." In this phrase God's unity (*tawhid*) is emphasized. God is one. He is neither begotten nor does he beget . . . Nothing can be compared to Him. Nothing is like Him. The greatest sin in Islam is therefore *shirk*, or "association"—the act of putting someone or something on a par with or ahead of God. All idolatry is rejected. Muslims reject also any anthropomorphic representation in religious practice and art, lest that become a substitute for God. . . .

The transcendent unit of God does not, however, mean that God is remote to the believer. God is always active in His world through His mercy and grace . . . On the day of final judgement, when each person is held accountable before God, even there God's mercy will prevail so that salvation cannot be earned by human effort but rather is ultimately dependent upon the mercy of God . . .

The Qur'an—God's Self-Revelation
How has this transcendent God made His will known to His people? The Islamic answer is the *Qur'an*, which is the word of God. The word *Qur'an*, means "recitation" or "reading". It refers directly to the manner of revelation. . . . Muslims believe that the *Qur'an* contains the exact words recorded and transmitted without error that God spoke in heaven . . .

From this understanding of the origin of the *Qur'an*, a number of other concepts flow. Because it is God's word, the *Qur'an* is without error. That which disagrees with it is *ipso facto* wrong. Though Muslims believe that God has given revelations to earlier prophets, specifically to Moses in the Law, to David in the Pslams, and to Jesus in the Gospel, nevertheless these earlier writings have been so corrupted by Jews and Christians that they have validity only when they confirm that which the *Qur'an* maintains. In areas of difference, the inerrancy of the *Qur'an* prevails. To believe otherwise would be to dishonor God by attributing error to Him . . .

The Prophethood of Muhammad
Crucial to an adequate understanding of Islam is an appreciation of the role of the Prophet Muhammad. Muhammad (570-632 A.D.) was born in Meccah, the commercial and cultural center of the Arabian peninsula at that time. At the age of forty, he began to receive revelations from God which he recited to the people of Meccah. Many of these early revelations were warnings about God's judgement upon the pagan religious practices and the social injustice which characterized the life of that city. These revelations were a call for the people to repent of their evil ways and to return to the worship of the one true God. Such announcements earned for Muhammad the wrath of those in Meccah who maintained their positions of power and authority by means of these evil conditions. When all appeared to be lost, the Prophet received from the people of Yathrib, a city some 200 miles to the north of Meccah, an invitation for him and his small group of followers to come and exercise leadership in their city. The invitation was accepted . . . In Yathrib, though not without difficulty, Islam took root and grew, expanding eventually beyond the bounds of Yathrib to encompass the city of Meccah and the whole of the Arabian peninsula. The rise and spread of Islam validates for the Muslim the Prophet's message.

Islamic Community
From the point of view of modern events, the Islamic understanding [of community] needs special attention. Those who do Islam are united into the community of the faithful. This community is that which must bear responsibility for the success or failure of the Islamic witness . . .

102

The community preserves its unity not only in the performance of [Islamic obligatory practices] but also in common obedience to an even larger of body of law, called the *Shariah*, the "way", or "right path." In its totality it is the complete embodiment of God's guidance for his community. The sources of the *Shariah* lie first of all in the *Qur'an*. Then in the Sunnah of the Prophet, and finally in a codification of legal interpretation that took place within the first three centuries after the death of the Prophet. During this time, four major schools of jurisprudence developed. . . .

The *Shariah* defines for Muslims what faithfulness to God entails and the blessings that will result. . .All the moral and ethical principles needed for wholesome community life, all aspects of the individual's own conduct within the community are guided by the legal provisions of the *Shariah*. Obedience to these provisions insures equality among all people and a society that is just. . . .

Since the well-being of the community is dependent upon the obedience of the community to *Shariah*, it is only natural that Muslims ensure the wellbeing of their community against their faithfulness to the *Shariah*. Therefore it is the obligation of Muslim governments [like Pakistan] to see that a Muslim nation rules itself by the *Shariah* law . . .

Like the adherents of every other religious community and tradition, Muslims too will, on occasion, fail to live up to their ideals or use religious ideals to achieve selfish ends. In either case, they deny their Islam. Religious claims, when judged true, have, however, the characteristic of spreading beyond the failures or successes of one generation of believers to appeal afresh to later generations. Such has been the case with Islam. Therefore its faith and practice must be taken seriously by all who in their own way have responded to the divine call to faithfulness. Anything less would be a denial of God.

APPENDIX II

Witness and Dialogue

Christians occasionally struggle between their call to witness to the Gospel and their desire to respect the integrity of other faiths. What follows is the way one U.S. denomination has brought these two convictions into harmony. (From "Called to be Neighbors and Witnesses" Guidelines for Interreligious Relationships, prepared by the Division of Education and Cultivation of the General Board of Global Ministries, United Methodist Church, adopted by the 1980 General Conference of the United Methodist Church.)

For some Christians, it seems strange even to refer to "persons of other faiths." We are accustomed to calling them "non-Christians" or "non-believers." These attitudes have developed out of confidence in the ultimate truth of our own faith and from ignorance of and insensitivity to other faiths, to the truth they contain, and to the profound meaning and purpose they give to the lives of people.

In conversation with a lawyer (Luke 10:25), Jesus reminded him that his neighbor, the one to whom he should show love and compassion, included a stranger, a Samaritan. Today, our Lord's call to neighborliness (Luke 10:27), includes the "strangers" of other faiths who have moved into our towns and cities. It is not just that historical events have forced us together. The Christian faith itself impells us to love our neighbors of other faiths and to seek to live in contact and mutually beneficial relationships, in community, with them.

What does it mean to be a neighbor? It means to meet other persons, to know them, to relate to them, to respect them and to learn about their ways which may be quite different from our own. It means to create a sense of community in our neighborhoods, towns and cities and to make them places in which the unique customs of each group of people can be expressed and their values protected. It means to create social structures in which there is justice for all and in which everyone can participate in shaping their life together "in community." Each race or group of people are not only allowed to be who they are, but also their way of life is valued and given full expression.

Christians distinguish several meanings of "community." One definition expresses their relationships as members of one another in the body of Christ, the Church, a people called together by Christ, a "communion of saints" who look to the reign of God. A broader definition points to the relationship that is shared with others in the wider human community, where Christians are concerned for peace, justice and reconciliation for all people. Other faiths also have their understanding of "community." The vision of a "worldwide community of communities" commends itself to many Christians as a way of being together with persons of different faiths in a pluralistic world. That suggests that we United Methodist Christians, not just individually, but corporately are called to be neighbors with communities of other faiths (Buddhist, Jewish, Muslim, Hindu and others), and to work with them to create a human community, a set of relationships between people at once interdependent and free, in which there is love, mutual respect and justice.

Called to be Witnesses

Within this religiously diverse community, Christians, trusting in Jesus Christ for their salvation, are called to witness to him as Lord to all people (Acts 1:8). We witness to our Lord through words which tell of his grace, through deeds of service and social change that demonstrate his love, and through our life together in the Christian community, exhibiting God's power to heal, reconcile and unite.

. . . As we United Methodist Christians reflect anew on our faith and seek guidance in our witness to and encounter with our new neighbors, we rediscover that God who has acted in Jesus Christ for the salvation of the whole world, is also Creator of all humankind, the "one God and Father of all, who is Lord of all, works through all, and is in all," (Eph. 4:6 TEV). The God to whom we point in Jesus Christ is the God who is at work in every society in ways we do not fully understand and who has not left himself without witness in any human community. Here Christians confront a profound mystery, the awareness of God who is related to all creation and at work in the whole of it, and the experience of God who has acted redemptively for the whole creation in Jesus Christ. Christians witness to God in Jesus Christ in the confidence that here all people find salvation and in the trust that because of what we know of God in Jesus, God deals graciously and lovingly with all people everywhere.

Dialogue

"Dialogue" is the word which has come to signify a different approach to persons of other faiths, one which takes seriously both the call to witness and the command to love and be neighbors and sees witnessing and neighborliness as interrelated activities. Rather than a one-sided address, dialogue combines witnessing with listening. It is the intentional engagement with persons of other faiths for mutual understanding, cooperation and mutual learning.

. . . In dialogue, one individual or group may seek relationship with another in order to expose misunderstandings and stereotypes and to break down barriers that separate and create hostility and conflict. Ethnic or religious communities may approach each other in dialogue in order to resolve particular problems or to foster cooperation in dealing with a local, national or even global situation of human suffering. At its deepest level, dialogue is both learning about and sharing our respective faiths. Each partner learns from the rich store of wisdom of the other, and each expresses his or her own deepest conviction in the faith that it has a truth worth sharing with the other.

Through dialogue with persons of other faiths, new insights are received regarding God's activity in the world today, the divine purpose for humankind as a whole, and the place of the Christian community within these purposes. It is also a common experience for Christians to feel the need to express their own faith with greater clarity. We can expect the Holy Spirit to make known new and different insights through our encounter with persons of other faiths.

The only precondition for dialogue is a willingness to enter a relationship of mutual acceptance, openness and respect. Effective dialogue requires that both partners have deep convictions about life, faith and salvation. True dialogue requires that Christians *not* suspend their fundamental convictions concerning the truth of the gospel but enter into dialogue with personal commitment to Jesus Christ and with the desire to witness to that faith. Effective dialogue also requires that Christians be open to persons of other faiths, to their convictions about life, truth and salvation and to their witness, as others also feel called to witness to their faith and teachings about the meaning of life.

An Exchange of Witness

Is not this urge to witness an obstacle to interreligious dialogue? It often has been, but it need not be. Where there is listening as well as speaking, openness and respect as well as concern to influence, there is dialogue *and* witness. Indeed, dialogue at its most profound level is an *exchange of witness*. Participants share with each other their perceptions of the meaning of life, of ultimate reality, salvation and hope, and the resources of their faith for enabling community. In genuine "dialogue," we "witness and are witnessed to." The most effective dialogue takes place when both sides really do care that the other hear, understand and receive the other's wisdom. Part of our witness is our openness to hearing the witness of the other.

Dialogue at these depths holds great promise. Long cherished convictions may be modified by the encounter with others. Misunderstanding may be clarified, potential hostilities reconciled, and new insights regarding one's own faith may emerge in contrast to that of another. The depths of another's faith may be so disclosed that its power and attractiveness are experienced. Dialogue is a demanding process, requiring thorough understanding of one's own faith and clear articulation of it to the other person.

Dialogue is *not* a betrayal of witness. Dialogue and witness are wrongly placed in opposition to each other. They need each other. Dialogue creates relationships of mutual understanding, openness and respect. Witness presses dialogue to the deepest convictions about life, death, and hope.

Many persons of other faiths are suspicious that dialogue is a new and more subtle tool for conversion. In some ways this is inevitable since Christians do want others to learn of and receive the truth and grace we know in Jesus Christ. The difference between dialogue and other forms of witness is that it is a context for learning from the other the truth and wisdom of the other faith as well as sharing with the other the truth and wisdom of our own. We leave to the Holy Spirit the outcome of our mutual openness. Our concern is to be obedient to our own call to witness and to the imperative to be loving and neighborly to persons of other faiths. In dialogue, these deeply held truths encounter each other in witness and love, so that larger wisdom and larger understanding of truth may emerge which benefit all parties in the dialogue. As we exhibit courtesy, reverence and respect and become neighbors, fears of each other are allayed, and the Holy Spirit works within these relationships.